Climate Monitoring in the Southwest Alaska Network

Annual Report for the 2009 Hydrologic Year

Natural Resource Technical Report NPS/SWAN/NRTR—2010/340

Chuck Lindsay

National Park Service
240 W 5th Avenue
Anchorage, Alaska 99501

June 2010

U.S. Department of the Interior
National Park Service
Natural Resource Program Center
Fort Collins, Colorado

The National Park Service, Natural Resource Program Center publishes a range of reports that address natural resource topics of interest and applicability to a broad audience in the National Park Service and others in natural resource management, including scientists, conservation and environmental constituencies, and the public.

The Natural Resource Technical Report Series is used to disseminate results of scientific studies in the physical, biological, and social sciences for both the advancement of science and the achievement of the National Park Service mission. The series provides contributors with a forum for displaying comprehensive data that are often deleted from journals because of page limitations.

All manuscripts in the series receive the appropriate level of peer review to ensure that the information is scientifically credible, technically accurate, appropriately written for the intended audience, and designed and published in a professional manner. This report received informal peer review by subject-matter experts who were not directly involved in the collection, analysis, or reporting of the data. Data in this report were collected and analyzed using methods based on established, peer-reviewed protocols and were analyzed and interpreted within the guidelines of the protocols.

Views, statements, findings, conclusions, recommendations, and data in this report are those of the author and do not necessarily reflect views and policies of the National Park Service, U.S. Department of the Interior. Mention of trade names or commercial products does not constitute endorsement or recommendation for use by the National Park Service.

This report is available from the Southwest Alaska Network Inventory and Monitoring website (http://science.nature.nps.gov/im/units/swan/) and the Natural Resource Publications Management website (http://www.nature.nps.gov/publications/NRPM).

Please cite this publication as:

Lindsay, C. 2010. Climate monitoring in the Southwest Alaska Network: Annual report for the 2009 hydrologic year. Natural Resource Technical Report NPS/SWAN/NRTR—2010/340. National Park Service, Fort Collins, Colorado.

NPS 953/103378, June 2010

Contents

Figures

Tables

Acronyms

ALAG	Alagnak Wild River
ANIA	Aniakchak National Monument and Preserve
ASOS	Automated Surface Observing System
AWOS	Automated Weather Observing System
BLM	Bureau of Land Management
BUOY	Moored Buoy (NOMAD)
CMAN	Coastal Marine Automated Network
COOP	Cooperative Observing Program
CRN	Climate Reference Network
ENSO	El Niño Southern Oscillation
FAA	Federal Aviation Administration
GOES	Geostationary Operational Environmental Satellites
GSFC	Goddard Space Flight Center
IPCC	Intergovernmental Panel on Climate Change
KATM	Katmai National Park and Preserve
KEFJ	Kenai Fjords National Park
LACL	Lake Clark National Park and Preserve
MODIS	Moderate Resolution Imaging Spectroradiometer
NASA	National Aeronautic and Space Administration
NCDC	National Climatic Data Center
NDBC	National Data Buoy Center
NESDIS	National Environmental Satellite, Data, and Information Service
NIFC	National Interagency Fire Center
NOAA	National Oceanic and Atmospheric Administration
NOMAD	Navy Oceanographic Meteorological Automated Device
NPS	National Park Service
NRCS	Natural Resources Conservation Service
NWS	National Weather Service
PDO	Pacific Decadal Oscillation
PRISM	Parameter-Elevation Regressions on Slopes Model
RAWS	Remote Automated Weather Station
SNOTEL	Snowpack Telemetry
SST	Sea Surface Temperature
SWAN	Southwest Alaska Network
USFS	United States Forest Service
WBAN	Weather Bureau Army Navy
WRCC	Western Regional Climate Center

Abstract

The Southwest Alaska Inventory and Monitoring Network monitors climate across a region that includes five national park units: Alagnak Wild River, Aniakchack National Monument and Preserve, Katmai National Park and Preserve, Kenai Fjords National Park, and Lake Clark National Park and Preserve. To date, monitoring efforts have focused on the placement and installation of new weather stations and the development, testing, and implementation of a protocol for monitoring climate. In addition to operating and maintaining nine weather stations in three network parks, weather observations are obtained from an additional 24 stations across the region of interest. This report, the first of an annual series, summarizes weather observations from the recent hydrologic year and provides a regional and historical climate context.

The Southwest Alaska Network region was colder and drier than average during the 2009 hydrologic year (October 2008 through September 2009). Compared to the climatological normal (the prevailing set of weather conditions calculated over a 30-year period, currently 1971-2000), annual mean temperatures for six long-term weather stations were -2.6 to +0.1 °F of normal. Total annual precipitation was 59 to 100% of normal. In general, precipitation across the Alaska Peninsula (western part of the region) was closer to average than precipitation across the Kenai Peninsula (eastern part). These colder and drier than average conditions are consistent with regional climatic conditions for the previous three years.

Three new weather stations were installed in two network parks during the 2009 hydrologic year. The Southwest Alaska Inventory and Monitoring Network installed a remote automated weather station on the coast of Katmai National Park and Preserve (Fourpeaked RAWS) and high in the Chigmit Mountains in Lake Clark National Park and Preserve (Chigmit Mountains RAWS). The National Oceanic and Atmospheric Administration installed a Climate Reference Network Station at Port Alsworth in Lake Clark National Park and Preserve (Port Alsworth 1 SW).

Acknowledgments

The author thanks all the dedicated park staff and volunteers who faithfully document weather and snowpack observations throughout the year. The author also thanks Leon Alsworth, Allen Gilliland, Vera Gilliland, Mark Kansteiner, Angela Olson, and Dale Vinson for their support and assistance with weather station installation and maintenance. The author credits Fritz Klasner for his many constructive suggestions, Nat Wilson for his work developing the data processing routines; and Bruce Giffen for all his dedication and efforts toward developing climate monitoring in Southwest Alaska Network parks. Careful reviews by Michael Shephard, Page Spencer, and John Papineau significantly improved earlier versions of this report.

Introduction

This report is the first of an annual series detailing the climate of the Southwest Alaska Network (SWAN). The purpose of these annual reports is to summarize observations from local weather stations for the recent hydrologic year and to provide a regional and historical context for these observations.

Climate Overview

The SWAN consists of five National Park Service units: Aniakchak National Monument and Preserve (ANIA), Alagnak Wild River (ALAG), Katmai National Park and Preserve (KATM), Kenai Fjords National Park (KEFJ), and Lake Clark National Park and Preserve (LACL). The climate of this region is largely influenced by the region's high latitude, proximity to oceans, complex topography, and the interaction of these features with global atmospheric circulation (Simpson et al. 2002). The park units in the SWAN are aligned along the northern Gulf of Alaska and the climate of the eastern, coastal areas of KATM, KEFJ, and LACL is maritime subarctic – characterized by moderate temperatures and abundant precipitation (Figure 1). Moist air masses are intercepted by the Kenai Mountains and the Aleutian and Alaska Ranges and heavy precipitation falls on their windward (east) sides. The western, more interior region of LACL is generally protected from maritime influence by large mountain ranges. The boreal climate here is more continental in nature – characterized by large annual range in temperature and a small annual range in precipitation. The climate of the park units on the Alaska Peninsula (ALAG, ANIA, and KATM) is transitional between polar (tundra climate) and maritime (maritime subarctic). In this region summer temperatures are moderated by the open waters of the Bering Sea (Bristol Bay), but winter temperatures are colder and more polar in nature due to the presence of sea ice in the coldest months. A more detailed discussion of the climate of the SWAN, including maps showing spatial and temporal patterns of temperature and precipitation, is provided by Redmond et al. (2005) and Davey et al. (2007).

Figure 1. Coastal regions of SWAN park units, like the East Arm of Nuka Bay in Kenai Fjords National Park, are characterized by moderate temperatures and abundant precipitation.

Climate vs. Weather

Although the terms climate and weather are sometimes used interchangeably, they differ in temporal perspective. Weather refers to the condition of the atmosphere at a specific point in time or during a short-lived atmospheric event. Climate refers to the aggregation of weather conditions for a location or region and can be defined with averages or representative values for weather elements.

Intrinsic Climate Variation

Fall and winter atmospheric circulation over the North Pacific Ocean is dominated by the Aleutian Low, which is important to the climatology of SWAN parks. Low pressure systems moving from west to east along the polar front usually reach maximum intensity in the area of the Aleutian Low, a semi-permanent low pressure center. Winter storm tracks generally follow the Aleutian Islands and move into the Gulf of Alaska with a frequency of about four to five storms a month where they affect SWAN parks with precipitation and strong winds. The Aleutian Low weakens in the summer season and summer storm tracks generally follow the Aleutian Islands and then turn northward into the eastern Bering Sea with a frequency of three to four storms per month (Simpson et al. 2002). The seasonal variability in the location and intensity of the Aleutian Low and associated storm tracks explains much of the seasonal variability in climate patterns and differences in the timing of maximum precipitation in SWAN parks (Bennett et al. 2006).

Annual to decadal climate variability in the SWAN is primarily influenced by large-scale changes in atmospheric and oceanic circulation, such as the El Niño Southern Oscillation (ENSO) and the Pacific Decadal Oscillation (PDO). The ENSO affects the strength and positioning of the Jet Stream and the PDO affects North Pacific sea level pressure and sea surface temperature. Although not completely understood, both climatic oscillations are recognized to have important climatic consequences to coastal Alaska, including the SWAN. ENSO events (El Niño and La Niña) are recognized to influence temperatures by ±2-4 °F at a large spatial scale (Simpson et al. 2002, Papineau 2005). The PDO is correlated with winter temperatures anomalies across Alaska; however, it has a stronger, more local influence on precipitation that primarily affects coastal areas. The PDO also influences winter time storm tracks, diverting them northward into the Cook Inlet area (Simpson et al. 2002).

Climate Change

The Intergovernmental Panel on Climate Change (IPCC) Fourth Assessment Report summarized the evidence that the global climate is changing rapidly and that rates of change are dramatically accelerated at northern latitudes. Alaska has warmed substantially over the 20th century, annual precipitation has increased (Weller et al. 1999), and the growing season has lengthened (Keyser et al. 2000). Temperature data from two long-term climate stations in the SWAN region show a significant increase in both mean winter temperatures and mean annual temperatures for 1949-2008 (Alaska Climate Research Center, 2009). Mean winter temperatures at King Salmon have increased by 8.1 °F and mean annual temperatures have increased by 3.8 °F. Mean winter temperatures at Homer have increased by 6.3 °F and mean annual temperatures have increased by 4.0 °F. While it is important to note that these temperature trends span the 1976-1977 Pacific Climate Shift (Hartman and Wendler 2005), the observed warming trend is supported by independent observations of sea ice, glaciers, permafrost, vegetation, and snow cover. Climate projections derived from five General Circulation Models based on an intermediate climate change scenario (IPCC-A1B) indicate that average annual temperatures for SWAN parks will increase by 0.9-1.1 °F per decade (Scenarios Network for Alaska Planning 2008). Precipitation is also generally projected to increase with 11-26% more snowfall in winter and 10-12% more rain in summer. It appears that the most severe environmental stresses in Alaska at present are climate related.

Other Resources

Those interested in additional climate-related information for the SWAN and surrounding areas should seek:

- Alaska Center for Climate Assessment & Policy (http://www.uaf.edu/accap/)
- Alaska Climate Research Center (http://climate.gi.alaska.edu/)
- Alaska Snow Water and Climate Services (http://ambcs.org/)
- Alaska State Climate Center (http://climate.uaa.alaska.edu/)
- National Climatic Data Center (http://www.ncdc.noaa.gov/oa/)
- NOAA Climate Services (http://www.climate.gov)
- National Data Buoy Center (http://ndbc.noaa.gov)
- National Weather Service – Alaska Region (http://www.arh.noaa.gov/)
- Pacific River Forecast Center (http://aprfc.arh.noaa.gov/)
- Western Regional Climate Center (http://www.wrcc.dri.edu/)

Methods

Stations

There are very few climate stations in the SWAN region that have long-term and reliable records. A complete inventory of land-based weather and climate monitoring stations in the SWAN was completed by Davey and others (2007). Climate conditions have been monitored at just a few locations near SWAN park units since the late 1930s and 1940s (one station record extends to 1908). Thirty three stations operated by six different climate monitoring programs are currently monitored by the SWAN (Figure 2). General descriptions of these climate monitoring programs are provided in Table 1 and station metadata are documented in Table 2. Collectively, these programs provide consistent monitoring of weather conditions and, in some cases provide a long-term climate record. In addition to operating and maintaining nine of these weather stations, the SWAN monitoring strategy is to obtain weather observations from agency archives annually, convert observations to daily and monthly summaries in both U.S. customary and metric units using customized routines, and store data on the SWAN server for ease of access and use.

Data Acquisition, Quality Control, and Data Processing

Six different climate monitoring programs (Table 1) maintain the official repositories for climate data monitored by the SWAN. Acquisition of climate data and data processing details are provided in the Methods for Monitoring Climate in SWAN Parks (Giffen et al., *in review*). In short, Remote Automated Weather Station (RAWS) data are obtained from the Western Regional Climate Center (WRCC). Data for National Weather Service Cooperative Observing Program (COOP), Automated Surface Observing System (ASOS), Automated Weather Observing System (AWOS), and Climate Reference Network (CRN) stations are obtained from the National Climatic Data Center (NCDC). Snow Course and Snowpack Telemetry (SNOTEL) data are obtained from the National Resources Conservation Service (NRCS). Coastal-Marine Automated Network (CMAN) and moored buoy data (BUOY) data are obtained from the National Data Buoy Center (NDBC). Data from ancillary stations (e.g. ranger stations, field data loggers) are not monitored by SWAN or included in this report.

Data quality control procedures are provided by the external agencies that manage the six different climate monitoring programs. Data-quality flags indicate missing or suspect data and the use of estimation procedures. RAWS data are subjected to additional data quality control that employs domain checks, which follow MesoWest, or more conservative, specifications.

After acquisition, climate data (excluding Snow Course data) are processed using routines that convert data to a standardized format in both metric and U.S. customary units. Climate variables are summarized to daily and monthly measures. Maximum, minimum, and arithmetic means are derived for temperature. Arithmetic means are derived for relative humidity and snow depth. Cumulative values are calculated for precipitation and solar radiation. Scalar and unit vector averaging are used to derive average wind speed and wind direction, respectively. Missing, suspect, or otherwise flagged data are not used for summary purposes. For all derived measures, the percentage of valid observations is reported as a measure of the reliability of the derived mean and cumulative values. Monthly measures should not be considered representative of actual climatic conditions if more than 10% (three days) of observations are missing or suspect. Yearly measures should not be considered representative if more than 17% (five days) are missing from any month.

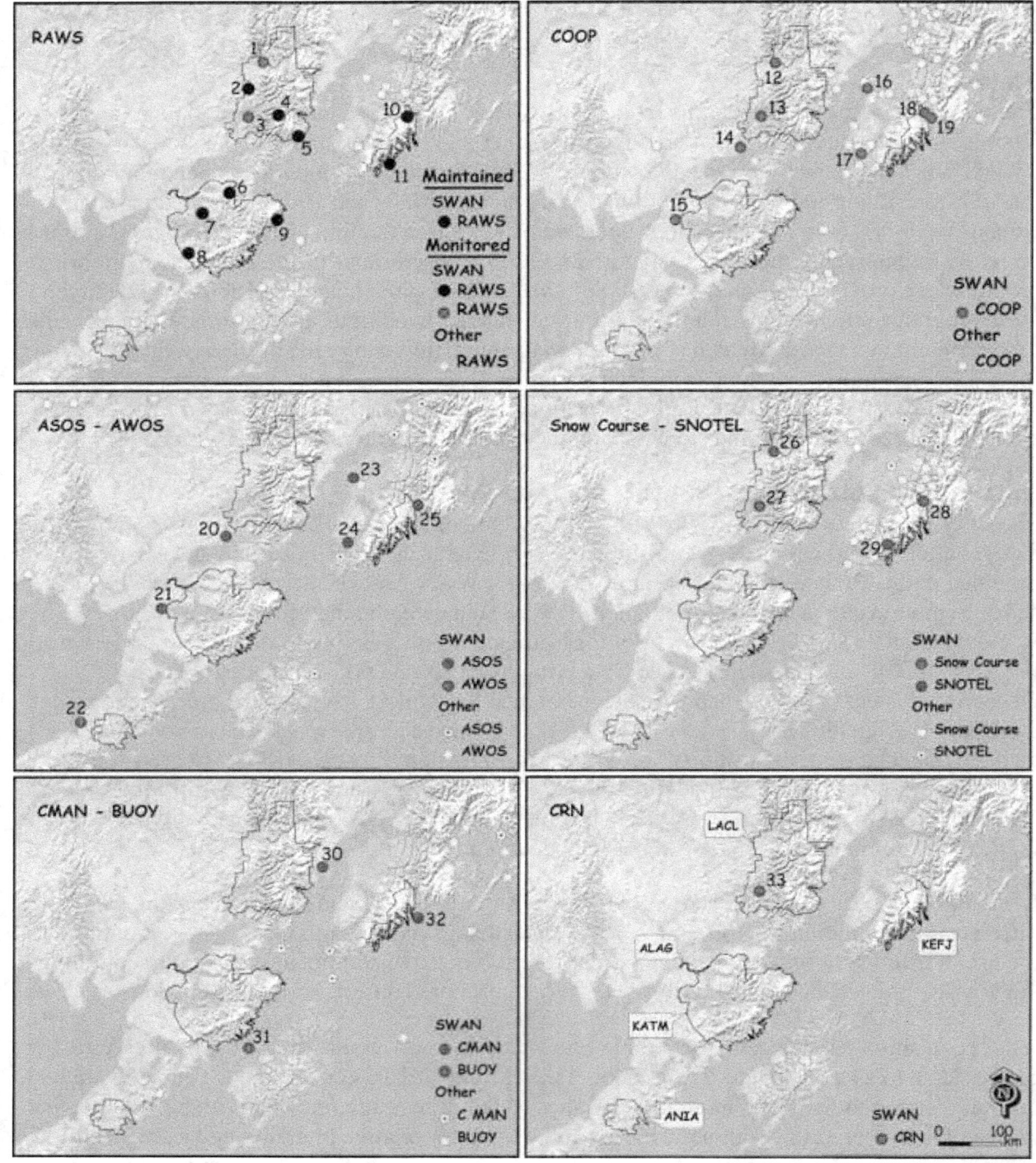

Figure 2. Locations of active climate stations in the six climate-monitoring programs in the SWAN region. Climate stations operated and maintained by the SWAN are shown in black. Additional stations that are monitored by the SWAN are shown in both black and red. See Table 1 for definitions of the climate-monitoring program acronyms. The numbers are used to identify each station in Table 2. Refer to the introduction for definitions of park-unit acronyms.

Table 1. Climate monitoring programs used for monitoring climate in the SWAN. Numbers in parentheses indicate the numbers of stations located within park boundaries – numbers outside of parentheses indicate stations located outside, but nearby, park boundaries.

Climate monitoring program (Acronym in bold)	Responsible agency	Program synopsis	No. stns. monitored
RAWS (Remote Automated Weather Stations)	National Interagency Fire Center (NIFC); NPS, BLM, USFS, etc.	Interagency network of weather stations mostly used by fire-personnel to estimate a fire-danger rating in support of preventative measures, and to forecast the behavior of wildland fires. Automated sensors record hourly air temperature, relative humidity, precipitation, wind speed and direction, solar radiation, and snow depth.	0 (11)
COOP (National Weather Service Cooperative Observing Program)	National Oceanic and Atmospheric Administration (NOAA)-National Weather Service (NWS)	Observer-based program created in 1890 to define the climate of the United States and help measure extreme weather events, climate variability, and long-term climatic changes. Manual observations include daily maximum and minimum air temperature, precipitation, and snowfall.	6 (2)
ASOS (Automated Surface Observing System); **AWOS** (Automated Weather Observing System)	NOAA-NWS; Federal Aviation Administration (FAA)	Weather stations installed at airports and military bases mostly used to support aviation needs and weather forecasting. Automated sensors record sub-hourly air temperature, relative humidity, precipitation, wind speed and direction, barometric pressure and other elements.	6 (0)
SNCO (Snow Course); **SNOTEL** (SNOwpack TELemetry)	National Resources Conservation Service (NRCS)	Observer-based program that manually measures snow depth and snow-water equivalent along permanent transects; Automated stations that provide hourly measurements of air temperature, precipitation, snow depth, snow-water equivalent and other elements.	1 (3)
CMAN (Coastal-Marine Automated Network); Moored **BOUY** (Navy Oceanographic Meteorological Automated Device or NOMAD)	NOAA-National Data Bouy Center (NDBC)	Weather stations installed at lighthouses, capes, beaches, nearshore islands, and offshore platforms. Automated sensors record hourly air temperature, wind speed, gust, and direction, barometric pressure. Some stations also measure sea water temperature, and wave direction and intensity. Moored buoys equipped with automated sensors that record hourly air temperature, wind speed and direction, barometric pressure and other elements.	3 (0)
CRN (Climate Reference Network)	NOAA-National Climatic Data Center; NOAA-Atmospheric Turbulence and Diffusion Division	Network of weather stations being developed to provide long-term observations of temperature and precipitation that can be coupled to long-term, historical observations for the detection and attribution of present and future climate change. Automated sensors record hourly air temperature and precipitation. Other elements include ground surface temperature, solar radiation, and wind speed.	0 (1)

Table 2. Weather stations monitored by the SWAN. Station names are those used by the climate monitoring network, but the acronyms are unique to this report. Map numbers refer to locations in Figure 1. The ID number is from the climate monitoring network (e.g. NESDIS ID, COOP Station No., WBAN ID, NRCS ID, NDBC No.). The station start is the earliest date listed for that ID number in the NCDC Multi-network Metadata System. Older climate data may be available from a station with the same name, but with a different ID number, and most likely reflect observations from a different type of weather station that may (or may not) have been located in the same location.

Station name	Acronym	Station type	Map No.	ID no.	Lat. N	Lon. W	Elev ft.	Station start
Chigmit Mountains	CHMO	RAWS	4	FA6544FC	60.2249	153.4675	4658	7/2009
Contact Creek	COCR	RAWS	8	32803738	58.2076	155.9225	657	6/2008
Coville	COVI	RAWS	7	3280B12C	58.8025	155.5629	1567	6/2008
Drift River Terminal	DRRI	CMAN	30	DRFA2	60.5533	152.1367	53	9/1999
Exit Glacier	EXGL	SNCO	28	49L18	60.1903	149.6212	400	9/1988
Fourpeaked	FOUR	RAWS	9	328135C2	58.7057	153.5179	1074	6/2009
Harding Icefield	HAIC	RAWS	10	FA656210	60.1325	149.7820	4335	7/2004
Hickerson Lake	HILA	RAWS	5	3280C7BC	59.9148	152.8925	1048	6/2008
Homer Airport	HOAI	COOP	17	503665	59.6428	151.4872	64	9/1949
Homer Airport	HOAI	ASOS	24	25507	59.6428	151.4872	64	12/1997
Iliamna Airport	ILAI	COOP	14	503905	59.7539	154.9069	183	9/1949
Iliamna Airport	ILAI	ASOS	20	25506	59.7539	154.9069	183	12/1997
Kenai Airport	KEAI	COOP	16	504546	60.5797	151.2391	91	9/1949
Kenai Airport	KEAI	ASOS	23	26523	60.5797	151.2391	91	5/1999
King Salmon Airport	KISA	COOP	15	504766	58.6829	156.6563	47	7/1955
King Salmon Airport	KISA	ASOS	21	25503	58.6829	156.6563	47	6/1998
McArthur Pass	MCPA	RAWS	11	3280244E	59.4726	150.3337	1266	6/2008
Nuka Glacier	NUGL	SNTE	29	50K06S	59.6943	150.7110	1250	10/1990
Pfaff Mine	PFMI	RAWS	6	FA65578A	59.1109	154.8367	2018	6/2008
Pilot Rock	PIRO	CMAN	32	PILA2	59.7417	149.4700	79	12/1999
Port Alsworth	POAL	COOP	13	507570	60.2033	154.3164	260	6/1960
Port Alsworth	POAL	SNCO	27	54L01	60.1921	154.3272	270	10/1991
Port Alsworth	POAL	RAWS	3	FA6102CC	60.1958	154.3200	321	6/1992
Port Alsworth 1 SW	P1SW	CRN	33		60.1958	154.3198	315	9/2009
Port Heiden	POHE	AWOS	22	25508	56.9500	158.6167	95	10/2007
Seward	SEWA	COOP	19	508371	60.1039	149.4439	110	9/1949
Seward Airport	SEAI	ASOS	25	26438	60.1283	149.4167	22	4/1997
Seward 8NW	S8NW	COOP	18	508375	60.1883	149.6275	410	6/1983
Shelikof Strait	SHST	BUOY	31	46077	57.9200	154.2542	0	10/2005
Snipe Lake	SNLA	RAWS	2	328041A8	60.6103	154.3199	2315	6/2008
Stoney	STON	RAWS	1	FA600036	61.0008	153.8958	1250	6/1992
Telaquana Lake	TELA	COOP	12		60.984	153.924	1250	6/1997
Telaquana Lake	TELA	SNCO	26	53L01	60.983	153.917	1550	8/1991

Reporting Interval

Reporting is based on the hydrologic year (October 1 to September 30) instead of the calendar year because it allows for more data completeness. Considerable data are not transmitted from many remote weather stations during winter months because of antenna icing (e.g. GOES telemetry); however these data are stored on-site, retrieved during subsequent summer months, and climate databases are then updated with the complete record. Additionally, the timing and seasonality of many physical processes that are driven by climate (e.g. onset and breakup of lake ice, glacial accumulation and ablation dynamics, and the magnitude and timing of streamflow) more closely follow the hydrologic year.

Summary Reports and Graphs

Summary reports and graphs for the most consistently measured climate variables from all weather stations monitored by the SWAN are included in the appendices and are organized by park, climate monitoring program, and station name. Daily measures are used for generating graphs (with the exception of NRCS Snow Courses) and monthly measures are used for generating summary reports. Mean temperature, total precipitation, mean snow depth, mean wind speed and direction, and maximum wind speed are presented in graphs. Minimum, maximum, and mean temperature data, the number of frost days (number of days where the minimum temperature is below freezing), and the number of ice days (number of days where the maximum temperature is below freezing) are included in the summary reports. Total precipitation, average snow depth, mean and maximum wind speed, maximum wind direction, and cumulative solar radiation are also presented in the summary reports. The percentage of valid observations is reported as a measure of the reliability of the derived mean and cumulative values for all reported climate variables. Climatic normal values (arithmetic mean over a 30-year interval) from the NCDC for the 1971-2000 period and period of record (POR) values from the WRCC are included for stations with a long enough observational record.

Analyses

The stations used for analysis in this summary report are the six weather stations with the longest, most complete records located near three SWAN parks that represent the major climate regimes in the network. These stations are Homer Airport, Iliamna Airport, Kenai Airport, King Salmon Airport, Port Alsworth, and Seward (Table 2).

Results

Regional Overview
Temperature

The SWAN region was colder than average during the 2009 hydrologic year. Compared to the climatological normal (the prevailing set of weather conditions calculated over a 30-year period, currently 1971-2000), annual mean temperatures for long-term weather stations in the SWAN region were -2.6 to +0.1 °F of normal (Table 3). The hydrologic year began with a significantly colder than normal fall across most of Alaska with the notable exception of the Arctic coast (Figure 3). Clear skies and cold temperatures generally dominated the SWAN region throughout the month of October and it was the 6th coldest October on record in Anchorage. Temperatures were also cooler than normal at King Salmon with one daily low temperature record being set (2 °F on October 22). November was also characterized by colder than normal temperatures along the western coast of the Gulf of Alaska with slightly higher than normal temperatures along the eastern coast (Figure 3). Particularly strong negative (colder) departures from normal were observed adjacent to the Bering Sea at locations that included Cold Bay and King Salmon. The month of November ranked as the 10th coldest November on record in King Salmon. December brought colder than normal conditions to the eastern SWAN region with warmer than normal temperatures in the western part (Figure 3). At most locations, the second half of December was significantly colder than the first half. Large temperature ranges were observed in the western SWAN region during December – King Salmon experienced a 66 °F temperature range (45 to -21 °F).

The entire SWAN region was also colder than normal during January, although a significant warming event occurred during the middle of the month. Anchorage experienced a 70 °F temperature change over a few days with a new daily high temperature record being set (50 °F on January 16). February was slightly colder than normal for most of the SWAN region (Figure 2) with near average conditions observed in King Salmon. March was also characterized by colder than normal conditions throughout the SWAN region. A cold snap affected much of the Alaska Peninsula during the later part of the month. April brought slightly colder than normal temperatures to most of the SWAN region, but a strong warming trend was observed as the month progressed. May was warmer than normal across the SWAN region (and most of Alaska) with several daily high temperature records being set (70 °F in Anchorage on May 2 and 73 °F in King Salmon on May 3). June brought near normal temperatures to most of the SWAN region. The SWAN region experienced higher than normal temperatures during July. The first half of the month was especially warm with three daily high temperature records in a row being set in Seward (e.g. 85 °F on July 6) and a high temperature of 80 °F observed in King Salmon (July 10 and 11). A cooling trend was observed across most of the SWAN region during the second half of the month. August was characterized by near normal or slightly colder than normal temperatures. The first frost was observed at several locations on the Alaska Peninsula, including King Salmon (on August 26, which is early for this location). September brought near normal temperatures to most of the SWAN region although two high temperature records were set in King Salmon during the middle of the month (65 °F on September 11). Most locations experienced multiple frosts in September and snow fell in Port Alsworth near the end of the month.

Precipitation

Most of the SWAN region was drier than average during the 2009 hydrologic year. Compared to the climatological normal, total annual precipitation at long term weather stations in the SWAN region was 59 to 100% of normal (Table 4). In general, precipitation across the western part of the SWAN region (Alaska Peninsula) was closer to average than precipitation across the eastern part of the SWAN region (Kenai Peninsula, Figure 5). October was characterized by drier than normal conditions across most of the Kenai Peninsula, especially in Seward where precipitation was 57% of average. Snowfall for the month was above normal in Anchorage, but half of the normal amount in King Salmon and the ground was snow free by the start of November. November was drier than normal across the entire SWAN region; however, snowfall was above normal in Anchorage and King Salmon with twelve and four inches remaining on the ground at the end of the month, respectively. December was also drier than normal with slightly above average snowfall across the SWAN region. Eighteen inches of snow fell in Anchorage and 12 inches fell in King Salmon with 17 and four inches remaining on the ground at the end of the month, respectively.

January was drier than normal across most of the SWAN region, with the notable exception of Pt. Alsworth, which received almost four inches of precipitation (water equivalent) – 377% of normal. Anchorage received 11 inches of snow and King Salmon received nine inches with 12 and five inches of snow remaining on the ground at the end of the month, respectively. Higher elevations across the SWAN region were at or below average snowpack. February brought drier than normal conditions to the eastern part and wetter than normal conditions to the western part of the SWAN region. Homer received 34% of normal precipitation while, in turn, King Salmon received 171% of normal precipitation (water equivalent). Fourteen inches of snow fell in Anchorage and 9 inches fell in King Salmon with 16 and one inch of snow remaining on the ground at the end of the month, respectively. The snowpack at higher elevations in the western part (Bristol Bay basin) and eastern part (Kenai Peninsula) of the SWAN region was below average, while the central part of the SWAN region (Cook Inlet basin) was at or slightly above average (NRCS, 2009). March continued the trend of drier than normal conditions in the eastern part and wetter than normal conditions in the western part of the SWAN region. Iliamna, Port Alsworth, and King Salmon all received above normal precipitation, while Homer, Kenai, and Seward were well below normal. Anchorage received 15 inches of snow and King Salmon received 30 inches (a monthly record for March) with a daily record setting seven inches of snow falling on March 23. Fourteen and seven inches of snow remained on the ground at the end of the month in Anchorage and King Salmon, respectively. The snowpack at higher elevations in the western and central SWAN region was near normal, but the snow pack at higher elevations in the eastern SWAN region remained below normal. April was characterized by drier than normal conditions across most of the SWAN region with long term stations receiving 17-99% of normal precipitation. Less than two inches of snow fell in Anchorage, however, eight inches fell in King Salmon, which is twice the normal amount. Only a trace of snow remained on the ground at the end of the month at both locations. The snowpack at higher elevations in the western and central SWAN region was slightly below normal and the snow pack at higher elevations in the eastern SWAN region was significantly below (<50%) normal. Drier than normal conditions prevailed during May although conditions were closer to the climatological normal with long term stations receiving 27-117% of normal precipitation. No snowfall was observed in Anchorage or King Salmon.

Table 3. Average daily temperatures during hydrologic year 2009 (Oct. 1, 2008 to Sep. 30, 2009) and departures from 1971-2000 averages for select SWAN region stations.

Station name	Station ID	Oct	Nov	Dec	Jan	Feb	Mar	Apr	May	Jun	Jul	Aug	Sep	Annual
Homer Airport	503665	34.5 (-3.3)	26.9 (-2.5)	23.8 (-2.0)	20.5 (-2.9)	22.1 (-2.8)	26.4 (-3.0)	36 (-0.4)	44.3 (0.6)	49.4 (-0.6)	54.6 (0.5)	52.8 (-1.0)	47.6 (-0.3)	36.7 (-1.4)
Iliamna Airport	503905	29.2 (-5.4)	18.2 (-6.7)	22.8 (3.7)	12.4 (-4.0)	15.4 (-1.0)	15.3 (-7.5)	30.1 (-2.2)	45.5 (-2.4)	50.1 (-0.8)	56.2 (0.4)	54.3 (-0.2)	47.5 (-0.1)	33.3 (-1.6)
Kenai Airport	504546	31.6 (-2.7)	22.6 (0.8)	13.4 (-2.9)	10.5 (-2.9)	15.2 (-1.4)	21.3 (-2.2)	35.2 (0.6)	47.2 (2.8)	52.5 (1.7)	57.4 (2.4)	55.4 (1.4)	49.7 (2.8)	34.4 (0.1)
King Salmon Airport	504766	28.6 (-4.7)	14.8 (-8.4)	20.8 (3.6)	10.7 (-4.7)	16 (0.4)	18.1 (-5.4)	32.3 (-0.8)	45.5 (2.0)	50.5 (-0.4)	56.7 (1.0)	52.4 (-2.4)	47.1 (-0.5)	32.9 (-1.6)
Port Alsworth	507570	28.1 (-6.4)	16.4 (-7.5)	-- (--)	7.3 (-7.4)	13.4 (-2.7)	15.7 (-8.2)	34.1 (-0.8)	47.9 (2.1)	53.8 (-0.2)	60.5 (2.2)	-- (--)	48.6 (0.7)	-- (--)
Seward	508371	35.2 (-4.6)	27.9 (-3.8)	23.1 (-5.0)	21.1 (-5.1)	24.5 (-2.7)	28.3 (-3.7)	36.4 (-2.2)	45.9 (0.1)	50.7 (-1.4)	56 (-0.4)	53.5 (-2.4)	48.5 (-1.1)	37.7 (-2.6)

Note: Temperatures are given in degrees Fahrenheit. Departures from 1971-2000 averages are given in parenthesis. Station IDs are from National Weather Service COOP stations. Monthly statistics are not reported if more than 10% of observations (three days) are missing. Annual statistics are not reported if more than 17% of observations (five days) are missing from any month. The percentage of valid observations are reported in the Appendices.

Table 4. Total monthly precipitation during hydrologic year 2009 (Oct. 1, 2008 to Sep. 30, 2009) and percentage versus 1971-2000 averages for select SWAN region stations.

Station name	Station ID	Oct	Nov	Dec	Jan	Feb	Mar	Apr	May	Jun	Jul	Aug	Sep	Annual
Homer Airport	503665	2.26 (82)	1.71 (60)	1.15 (38)	1.47 (56)	0.69 (34)	0.67 (37)	0.32 (26)	0.83 (78)	0.41 (43)	0.95 (66)	2.05 (90)	2.46 (73)	14.97 (59)
Iliamna Airport	503905	3.42 (110)	1.19 (53)	0.85 (51)	1.31 (98)	1.09 (111)	1.44 (140)	0.96 (99)	1.23 (97)	1.2 (78)	3.25 (137)	1.98 (46)	2.91 (67)	20.83 (83)
Kenai Airport	504546	2.63 (99)	0.34 (20)	0.37 (26)	1.36 (127)	0.54 (59)	0.38 (47)	0.11 (17)	0.68 (72)	0.95 (87)	1.15 (66)	2.3 (88)	1.48 (45)	12.29 (65)
King Salmon Airport	504766	2.7 (129)	0.74 (48)	1.7 (122)	1.06 (103)	1.23 (171)	1.52 (192)	0.64 (68)	1.1 (81)	2.12 (125)	2.72 (127)	1.68 (58)	2.26 (80)	19.48 (100)
Port Alsworth	507570	1.88 (137)	1.31 (105)	-- (--)	2.98 (377)	1.35 (233)	2.08 (320)	0.33 (69)	0.56 (117)	1.21 (132)	1.73 (124)	-- (--)	2.48 (119)	-- (--)
Seward	508371	5.57 (57)	3.48 (49)	1.16 (15)	9.2 (128)	1.04 (18)	1.19 (29)	2.00 (42)	1.26 (27)	1.66 (72)	9.95 (444)	3.72 (68)	3.59 (35)	43.82 (61)

Note: Percentages of monthly average precipitation versus 1971-2000 given in parentheses. Station IDs are from National Weather Service COOP stations. Monthly statistics are not reported if more than 10% of observations (three days) are missing. Annual statistics are not reported if more than 17% of observations (five days) are missing from any month. The percentage of valid observations are reported in the Appendices.

Figure 3. Mean monthly temperature departures from 1971-2000 averages for select ASOS stations during the 2009 hydrologic year. Figures are from the NCDC.

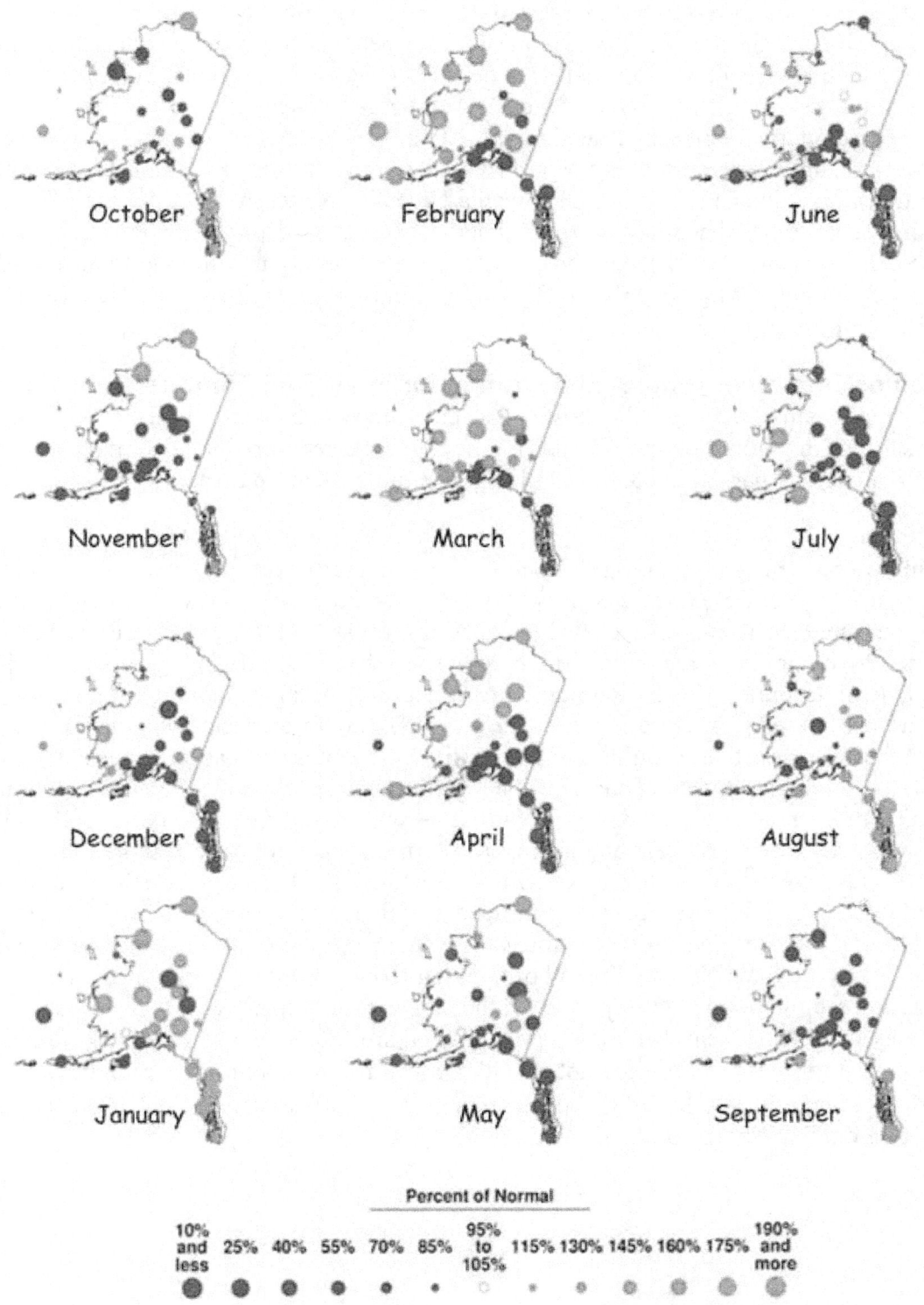

Figure 4. Total monthly precipitation percentages of 1971-2000 averages for select ASOS stations during the 2009 hydrologic year. Figures are from the NCDC.

Drier than normal conditions continued across the SWAN region through June, with less than half the normal monthly rainfall in Anchorage and Homer. Locations on the Alaska Peninsula were wetter with King Salmon and Port Alsworth reporting above normal precipitation. The first half of July was very dry across most of the SWAN region, however the second half of July saw significant precipitation along the coastline of the Gulf of Alaska and the month ranked as the second wettest July ever recorded in Seward (with almost 10 inches of rainfall, 444% of normal precipitation). Locations on the Alaska Peninsula were also wetter than normal with Iliamna, King Salmon, and Port Alsworth all reporting above average precipitation. Generally drier than normal conditions continued through the end of the hydrologic year with long term stations in the SWAN region reporting 46-90% and 35-119% of normal precipitation in August and September, respectively.

Location of Summary Reports and Graphs for Individual Stations

Summary reports and graphs for the most consistently measured climate variables from all weather stations monitored by the SWAN (Figure 2 and Table 2) are included in the appendices and are organized by park, climate monitoring program, and station name.

Limitations

Measuring winter-time precipitation (i.e. snowfall, snow depth, and snow water equivalent) is difficult to accomplish across the SWAN region. Snow surveys are relatively accurate, but they are only measured monthly and at a few key locations. Most remote weather stations have limited (photovoltaic) power supplies and therefore rely on unheated tipping buckets, which are only capable of accurately measuring liquid precipitation (e.g. rain). Although sonic snow depth sensors are used at many of these stations (e.g. RAWS), snow water equivalent is not measured. A few remote weather stations utilize storage or displacement precipitation gauges or snow pillows (Harding Icefield, Nuka Glacier). The logistical challenges and cost associated with maintaining these gauges or pillows (which are filled with an antifreeze solution) and protecting them from wildlife are significant and makes them impractical to operate at more than a few key locations. Undercatch (the difference between the actual amount of snow and the amount measured by a precipitation gauge) is a significant problem at the Harding Icefield because of the windy nature of the site. Currently, accurate year-round precipitation is only measured at a few locations within the SWAN, including all of the long term stations (Table 4) discussed above. Summarized precipitation values reported (in the tables in the appendices) for individual stations that are only capable of measuring liquid precipitation are denoted with an asterisk. Precipitation values reported for these stations are not considered valid if the maximum air temperature was below 31.1 °F and this is reflected in the percentage of valid observations that are reported as a measure of the reliability of cumulative values.

Discussion

Summary of 2009 Hydrologic Year
Temperature

Mean annual temperatures and total annual precipitation were below average across most of the SWAN region during the 2009 hydrologic year. May and July were the notable exception to generally cooler than normal conditions – mean monthly temperatures were warmer than average at all long-term stations except for Seward during these two months. Kenai observed above average mean monthly temperatures for six consecutive months beginning in April, 2009 and was the only long-term station to observe mean annual temperatures that were close to the climatological normal. Temperature summaries for long-term stations are presented relative to climate maps derived from the Parameter-Elevation Regressions on Slopes Model (PRISM) in Figure 5. The PRISM model uses point climate station data (climatological normals) and a digital elevation model to generate gridded interpolations of temperature and precipitation. Climate maps derived from PRISM data provide a useful spatial reference for the interpretation of patterns of variability in climate data.

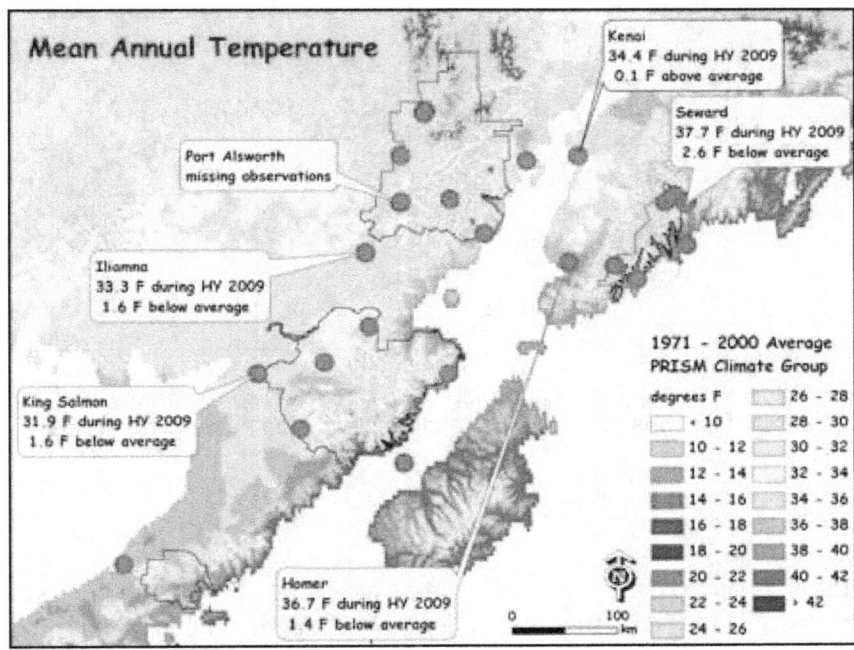

Figure 5. Mean annual temperatures (2009 hydrologic year) for long-term stations in the SWAN region relative to spatially interpolated mean annual temperatures for the climatological normal (1971-2000) generated by the PRISM.

Precipitation

There was a clear pattern in the spatial distribution of precipitation with long-term stations in the western part of the SWAN region (Bristol Bay basin) generally receiving more precipitation than those located in the central and eastern part of the SWAN region. However, total annual precipitation at all long-term stations was at or below the climatological normal. Only late winter (February and March) and the middle of summer (July) yielded above average precipitation at most long-term stations. Precipitation summaries for long-term stations are presented relative to climate maps derived from the PRISM in Figure 6.

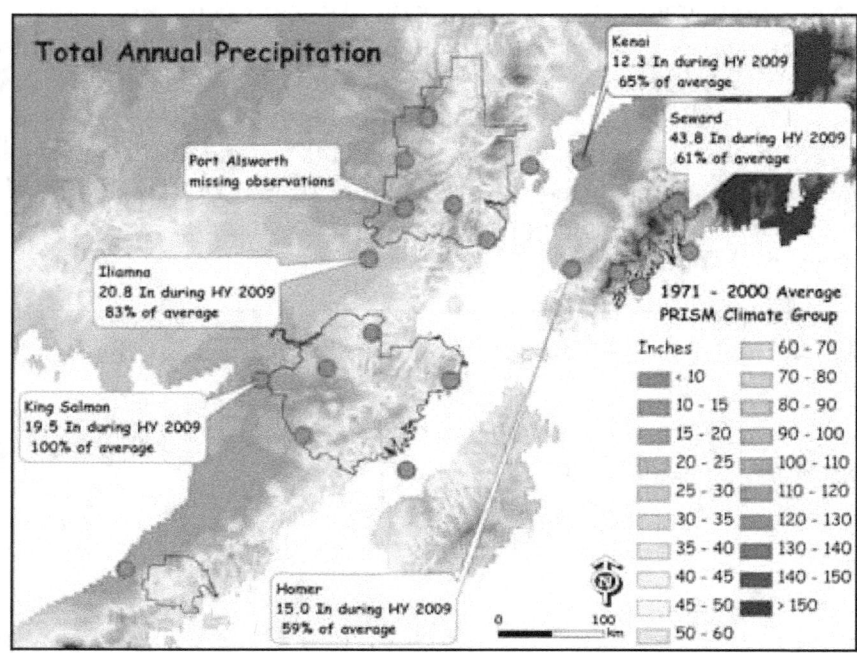

Figure 6. Total annual precipitation (2009 hydrologic year) for long-term stations in the SWAN region relative to spatially interpolated mean annual precipitation for the climatological normal (1971-2000) generated by the PRISM.

Historical Context
Cautionary Note

Assessments of the historical context of trends and average conditions for SWAN region weather stations should be viewed in the context of the available record. The approximately 50-year observational period for the long-term stations discussed above provides an adequate basis for evaluating the historical context of the recent climate with respect to climatological normals, but this period may be too short for discerning long-term changes in climate regimes. Although the climate data for the long-term stations discussed above has been subjected to a suite of quality assurance checks (NCDC, 2010), it has not been adjusted for bias resulting from historical changes in instrumentation and observing practices. Therefore, long-term climate trends are not calculated or reported here.

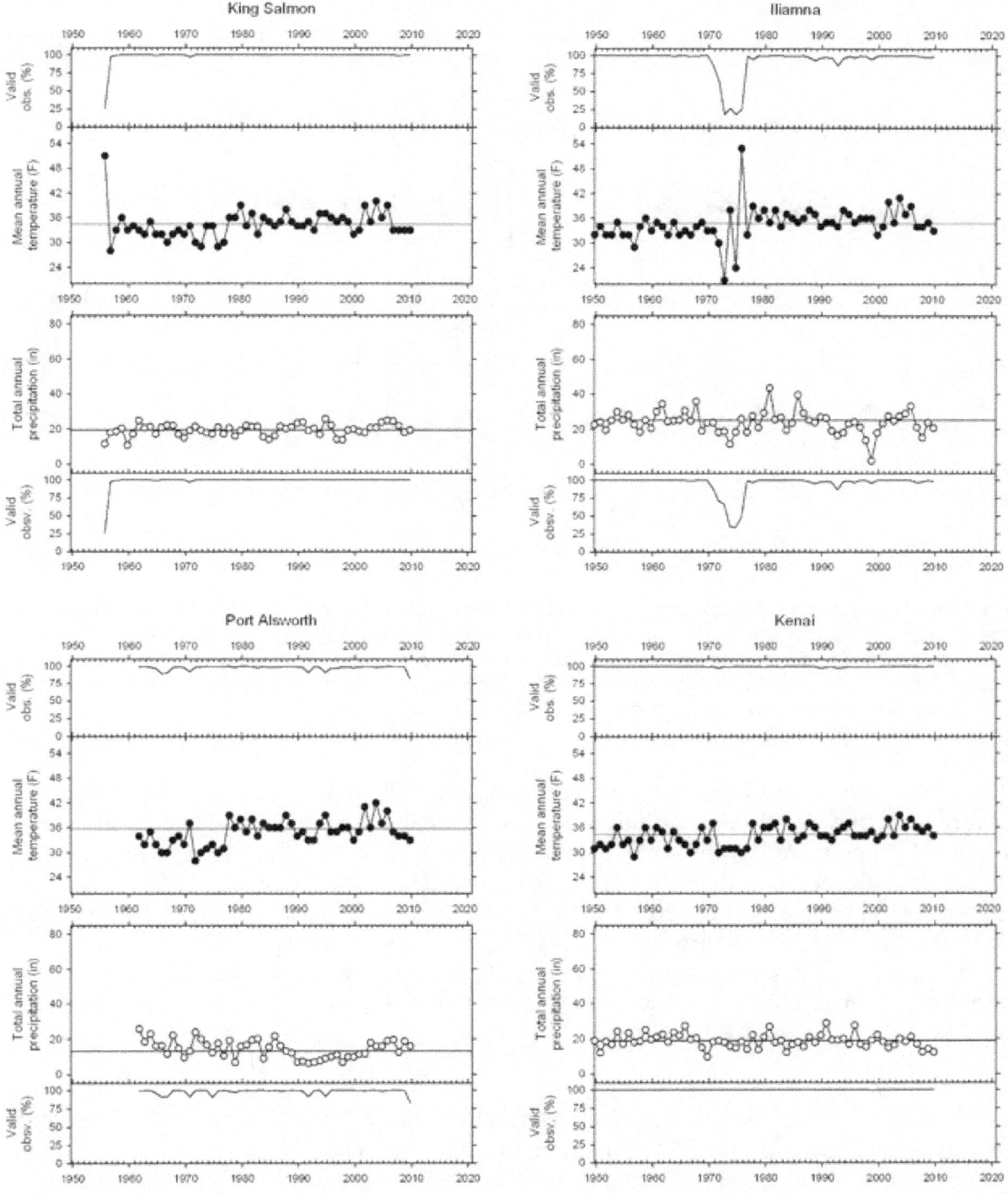

Figure 7. Mean annual temperature and total annual precipitation from 1950 to present for long-term weather stations in the SWAN region. The reporting interval is based on the hydrologic year. The horizontal reference lines reflect the climatological normal, the prevailing set of weather conditions calculated over a 30-year period, currently 1971-2000. The percentage of valid observations is reported as a measure of the reliability of the derived mean and cumulative values. Note that anomalous temperature and precipitation values (e.g. King Salmon 1955 and Iliamna 1971-1976) result from a low percentage of valid observations (e.g. missing winter temperature data will result in an artificially high mean annual temperature).

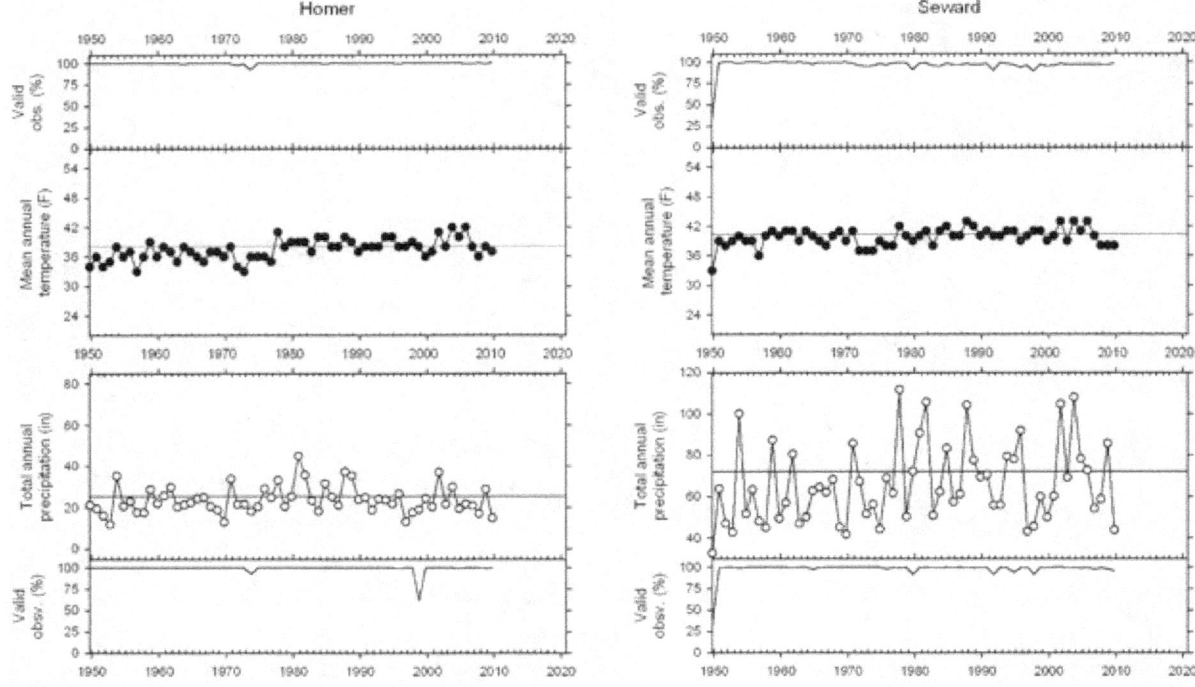

Figure 8. Mean annual temperature and total annual precipitation from 1950 to present for long-term weather stations in the SWAN region. The reporting interval is based on the hydrologic year. The horizontal reference lines reflect the climatological normal, the prevailing set of weather conditions calculated over a 30-year period, currently 1971-2000. The percentage of valid observations is reported as a measure of the reliability of the derived mean and cumulative values.

Assessment

Cooler than normal mean annual temperatures during the 2009 hydrologic year are consistent with recent temperatures observed during the previous three years (2006-2008 hydrologic years). Mean annual temperatures for the 2006-2009 hydrologic years were below average for all long-term stations except Kenai (Figures 7 and 8). The historical context for precipitation is less clear. Drier than normal total annual precipitation has generally been observed at Homer, Iliamna, and Kenai for at least the previous three years, and longer in Homer. Average, or above average precipitation has been observed in King Salmon and Port Alsworth for the last four years. Seward is characterized by wide interannual variability in precipitation over the entire period of record.

PDO Conditions

The 2009 hydrologic year was characterized by negative PDO conditions between October 2008 and August 2009, when positive PDO conditions developed (JISAO, 2010). These general (negative PDO) conditions were reflected by cold sea surface temperature (SST) anomalies in the Gulf of Alaska and Bering Sea (within a few hundred miles of shore) and warm SST anomalies in the central North Pacific (Figure 9). The position of the Aleutian Low and storm track is correlated with North Pacific SST anomalies; however, the impact of cooler SSTs alone for coastal areas may be significant as well. Differentiating between the effects of these two processes at an individual weather station is probably not possible.

Historically, an abrupt positive shift in mean annual temperature beginning during the 1977 hydrologic year is evident at five long-term stations (Kenai, King Salmon, Homer, Port Alsworth, and Seward) in the SWAN region (Figures 7 and 8). This shift is not noticeable at Iliamna, but is probably obscured by the poor observational record during the 1971-1977 hydrologic years (Figure 7). This climate shift has been well correlated with the shift from the negative to positive phase of the PDO (e.g. Simpson et al., 2002; Hartman and Wendler, 2005). Although it is not as pronounced as the shift in temperature, a corresponding positive shift in total annual precipitation is observed at Homer and Kenai (Figures 7 and 8). A general 10-40% increase in winter precipitation during the "positive" phase of the PDO has been observed at locations north of 57° N and on the Alaska Peninsula (Papineau, n.d.).

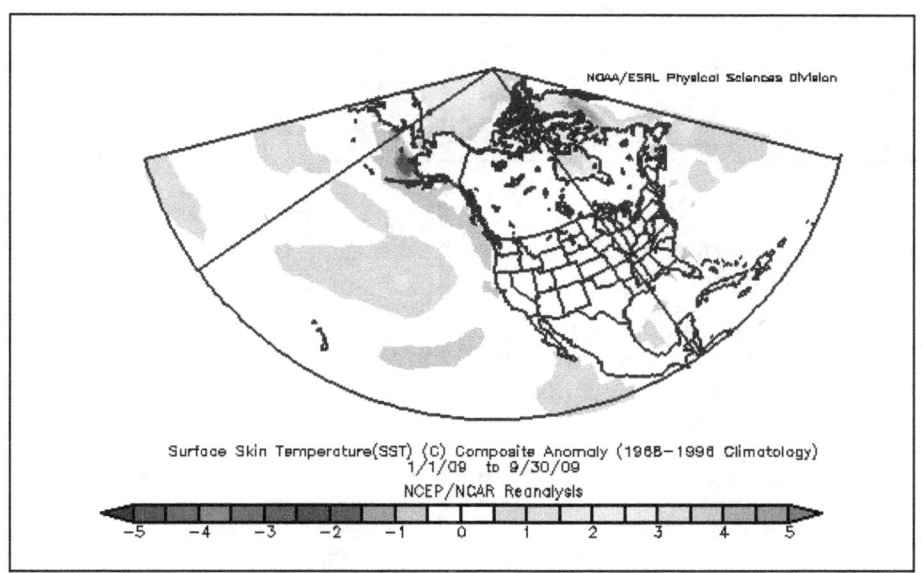

Figure 9. Sea surface temperature composite anomaly for the North Pacific area (January - September, 2009). Figure was generated using the NOAA Earth System Research Laboratory Physical Sciences Division daily mean composites plotting page using NCEP/NCAR reanalysis data. Climate means are based on 1968-1996.

ENSO Conditions

The 2009 hydrologic year was generally characterized by ENSO neutral conditions. Weak La Niña conditions developed during January and dissipated in March. El Niño conditions developed in June and persisted through September 2009. Significant annual variability in temperature and precipitation at long-term stations in the SWAN region may be attributed to fluctuations in the ENSO. Although the average El Niño event results in a modest increase in winter and summer temperatures across Alaska, the effect is highly variable both spatially (from one location to another) and temporally (from one El Niño event to another; Papineau, n.d.). The average La Niña event results in cooler than normal temperatures and drier conditions in both winter and summer. Temperature data from long-term stations in the SWAN region are weakly correlated to recent El Niño events (Table 5) with significantly warmer than average temperatures (compared to the climatological normal conditions) observed at all six stations during the 2003 and 2005 El Niño events. Temperature data from long-term stations in the SWAN region are also only weakly correlated to recent La Niña events with cooler than average temperatures (compared to the climatological normal conditions) observed at all six stations during the 1999 and 2000 La Niña events (Figures 7 and 8).

Table 5. El Niño and La Niña events (since 1950) of varying intensity listed by hydrologic year (NWS Climate Prediction Center, 2010).

El Niño events	El Niño events	La Niña events	La Niña events
1958	1988	1950	1974
1964	1992	1951	1975
1966	1995	1955	1976
1969	1998	1956	1985
1970	2003	1957	1989
1973	2005	1963	1996
1977	2007	1965	1999
1978		1968	2000
1983		1971	2001
1987		1972	2008

Other Climate Forcings

The colder and drier than normal conditions observed during the 2009 hydrologic year may be attributed to a higher than normal sea surface pressure anomaly in the greater Bering Sea region (Figure 10). When persistent ridging occurs in the North Pacific near the International Dateline during winter months, the polar jet stream is shifted south resulting in a major shift in the storm track across the North Pacific that typically results in cold, dry conditions across Alaska (Papineau, 2004).

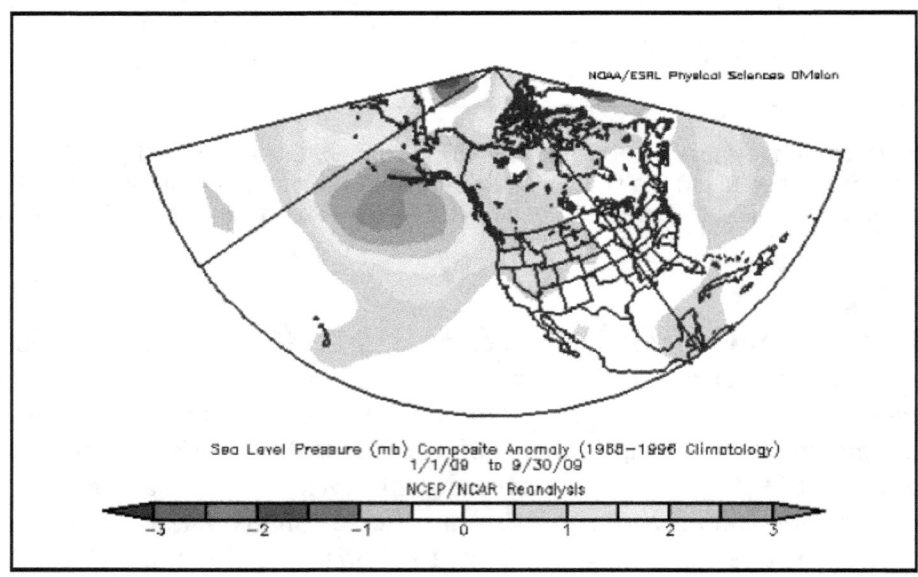

Figure 10. Sea level surface pressure composite anomaly for the North Pacific area (January - September, 2009). Figure was generated using the NOAA Earth System Research Laboratory Physical Sciences Division daily mean composites plotting page using NCEP/NCAR reanalysis data. Climate means are based on 1968-1996.

Climatic Extremes and Significant Weather Events

Climatic extremes were not quantified and are therefore not reported here, but will be included in future reports. Significant weather events that occurred at a large scale (i.e. across the SWAN region) during the 2009 hydrologic year included the following events. Pronounced cold snaps occurred in late November, early January and late December, early February, and late March. Mid-winter thaw events occurred in early December, mid-January, and mid-February. A significant mid-winter rain event occurred in mid-January. Noteworthy snowfall events occurred in mid-November, late December, late February, mid-March, and mid-April. Anomalously warm conditions were observed in mid-May, early June, and early July. Unseasonally high rainfall occurred in late July. Noteworthy strong wind events occurred in early October, early November, early December, mid January, mid-February, late March, late April, early and late June, late July, late August, and mid-September.

Ecological Relevance

Ecosystem connectivity is a key feature of the SWAN and a mechanistic understanding of the role of climate as an ecological determinant is the basis for monitoring climate. Climate drives the hydrologic cycle, affects hydrographic structure and circulation in ocean and lakes, affects primary production, influences wildlife habitat and forage, controls the timing of ecological processes, and influences the frequency and intensity of disturbances. Understanding the role of climate as a forcing agent is key to monitoring other vital signs monitored by the SWAN. Following are a few examples of how the recent climate has affected (and in one case been indirectly affected by) other physical systems in the SWAN region.

The 2009 hydrologic year saw a continuation of colder and drier than normal climatic conditions, which have generally persisted across the SWAN region for the last three to four years. Large lakes in the SWAN region froze earlier than in recent years in response to colder than average temperatures in October and November, the thinner than average snowpack experienced accelerated melting in spring and early summer because of volcanic ash cover, and the fire season was very active. Nonvianuk Lake on the Alaska Peninsula (Figure 11) froze (with >90% ice cover) on November 30, 2008 (NPS, unpublished data). Freeze-up dates for Nonvianuk Lake consistently occur in December during the relatively warm 2002–2006 hydrologic years, but occur in November during the cooler 2007-2009 hydrologic years (Spencer et al., 2008). A total of 19 eruptive events occurred at Redoubt Volcano over a 14-day period in March and early April of 2009 (Carlisle and Nelson, 2009). Volcanic ash from these eruptions was deposited over large parts of the SWAN region, specifically the Chigmit and Neacola Mountains (Figure 11) and parts of the Alaska and Kenai-Chugach Ranges. The ash reduced the albedo (reflectivity) of the snowpack thereby changing the timing and intensity of melting during late spring and early summer. This ash-on-snow event led to rapid melting of the already below-average snowpack. The combination of dry conditions, anomalously warm temperatures, and high pressure ridging in May and July was conducive to the spread of numerous wildfires on the Kenai Peninsula (Figure 11).

A number of strong wind events affected the SWAN region during the 2009 hydrologic year (Figure 12). These events were observed, to varying degrees, at weather stations located across the region. Most of these strong wind events occurred during cold months, when these events typically occur; however, two strong wind events happened during summer months, dramatically

23

affecting the hydrographic structure of large lakes in the SWAN region. Maximum wind gusts of 66.9 and 70.5 mph were observed at the Coville RAWS on on July 21 and 25, 2009 (Figure 12). Maximum wind speeds at the Port Alsworth RAWS reached 28.0 mph during both these events, significant in light of the sheltered location of this weather station. Deep vertical mixing of lake water at both Lake Clark and Naknek Lake was observed following these two wind events. Wind generated surface disturbance mixed warmer surface water with cooler, deeper lake water (Shearer and Moore, 2010).

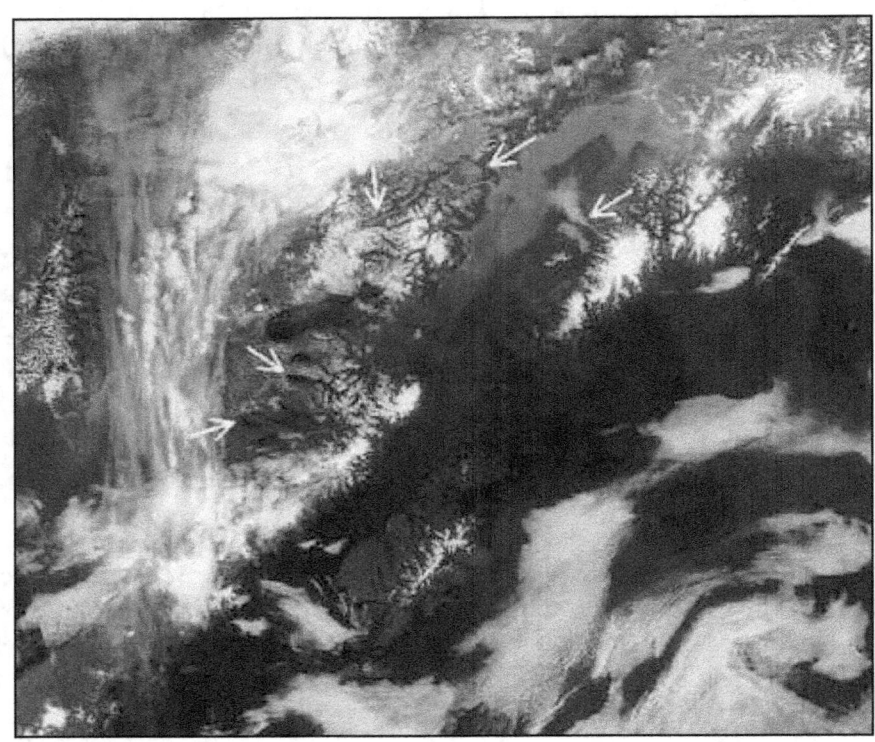

Figure 11. Satellite image of the SWAN region on July 9, 2009. The following features (discussed in the text) are marked with arrows (in order from left to right): large lakes including Naknek Lake, Nonvianuk Lake, and Lake Clark; ash deposited from Redoubt Volcano's eruptions covers most of the Neacola Mountains; a smoke column from a wildfire is visible north of Tustumena Lake. Aqua satellite image from NASA/GSFC, MODIS Rapid Response.

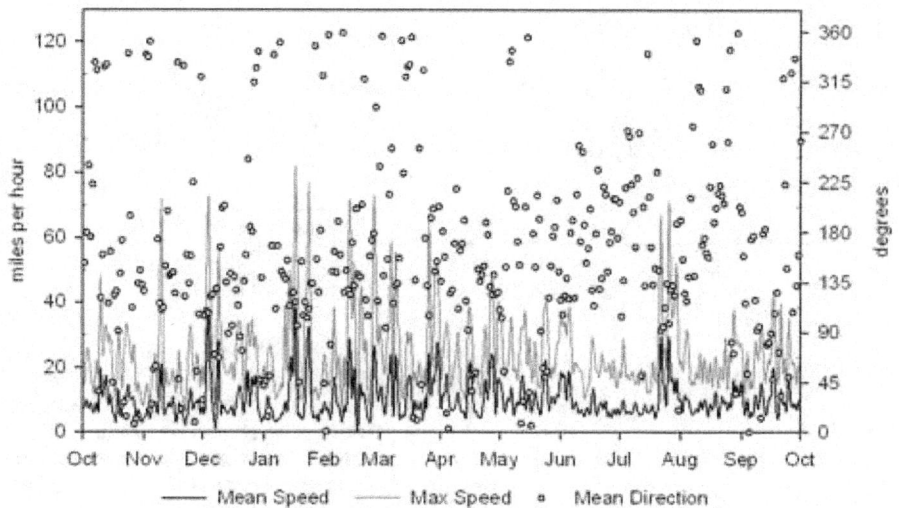

Figure 12. Mean and maximum daily wind speed and direction at the Coville RAWS during the 2009 hydrologic year. Nine strong wind events with gusts exceeding 60 mph were observed at this weather station. Seven of these events occurred in winter, when these events are more common. Two of these strong wind events occurred during summer, affecting the hydrographic structure of large lakes in the SWAN region, park operations, and visitor experience.

Status of Climate Monitoring in Network Parks

The SWAN installed two new weather stations in June 2009. The Fourpeaked RAWS was installed on the KATM coast and the Chigmit Mountains RAWS was installed in LACL. Annual maintenance was conducted on the seven remaining network RAWS in three parks. Three RAWS (Hickerson Lake, Snipe Lake, and McArthur Pass) were damaged by bears. Heavy duty conduit was subsequently installed at all low-elevation RAWS in order to protect sensor cables from wildlife encounters. A combination of strong winds and heavy icing broke the 20-foot masts that support the wind speed and direction sensors at both the Harding Icefield and McArthur Pass RAWS. These masts were replaced and additional guy wires were installed to support the masts at all high-elevation RAWS. A summary of all maintenance work at SWAN operated and maintained weather stations is presented in Table 6.

Accurately measuring winter-time precipitation (i.e. snowfall, snow depth, and snow water equivalent) continues to prove difficult to accomplish. Network RAWS rely on unheated tipping buckets, which are only capable of accurately measuring liquid precipitation (e.g. rain). Although sonic snow depth sensors are used at these stations, snow water equivalent is not measured. The sonic snow depth sensors are not performing well at high elevation and coastal weather stations because of the harsh environmental conditions at these sites. A displacement precipitation gauge (filled with an antifreeze solution) is used at the Harding Icefield RAWS. By design, this gauge is capable of accurately measuring winter-time precipitation. In reality, undercatch (the difference between the actual amount of snow and the amount measured by a precipitation gauge) is a significant problem because of the extremely windy nature of the site. Measured precipitation is only a fraction of the snow water equivalent reflected by the adjacent snowpack (15% over one year - based on observations made during the 2008 hydrologic year). A summary of all known issues affecting the performance and data quality of weather stations maintained and operated by the SWAN is provided in Table 7.

Table 6. Maintenance summary for RAWS operated and maintained by the SWAN. Acronyms are as follows: air temperature - relative humidity (AT/RH), wind speed (WS), wind direction (WD), solar radiation (SR), snow depth (SD), geostationary operational environmental satellite (GOES), data logger program (DLP), and soil temperature (ST).

Station	Date	Maintenance
Chigmit Mountains	06/30/2009	Installed station.
Contact Creek	06/23/2009	Scheduled maintenance. Replaced AT/RH sensor, installed heavy duty conduit for protection from wildlife, and installed additional cross-bracing on tower.
Coville	06/22/2009	Scheduled maintenance. Replaced AT/RH sensor, installed heavy duty conduit for protection from wildlife, and installed additional cross-bracing on tower.
Fourpeaked	06/09/2009	Installed station.
Harding Icefield	06/03/2009	Scheduled maintenance. Replaced AT/RH, WD, WS, SR, and SD sensors. Replaced GOES antenna. Serviced all-season precipitation gauge. Replaced 20 ft mast for wind sensors. Added guy lines to mast and installed additional cross-bracing on tower.
Hickerson Lake	06/29/2009	Scheduled maintenance. Considerable bear damage to station. Replaced AT/RH, SR, and GOES antenna. Installed heavy duty conduit for protection from wildlife and installed additional cross-bracing on tower.
McArthur Pass	10/31/2008	Unscheduled maintenance. Considerable bear damage to station. Switched GOES antenna to YAGI-type. Spliced cables back together.
McArthur Pass	06/02/2009	Scheduled maintenance. Replaced AT/RH, WS, and WD sensors. Replaced 20 ft mast for wind sensors. Added guy lines to mast. Installed heavy duty conduit for protection from wildlife and installed additional cross-bracing on tower.
Pfaff Mine	06/24/2009	Scheduled maintenance. Replaced AT/RH sensor. Installed heavy duty conduit for protection from wildlife and installed additional cross-bracing on tower.
Snipe Lake	06/27/2009	Scheduled maintenance. Replaced AT/RH sensor. Installed heavy duty conduit for protection from wildlife and installed additional cross-bracing on tower. Installed dual ST sensors. New DLP.

Table 7. Issues affecting performance and data quality of RAWS operated and maintained by the SWAN. Acronyms are as follows: relative humidity (RH), wind speed (WS), wind direction (WD), snow depth (SD), and soil temperature (ST).

Station	Date begin	Date end	Issue
Chigmit Mountains	10/01/2008	06/30/2009	Station not in operation yet
Chigmit Mountains	06/30/2008	09/30/2009	High precipitation recorded during strong wind events
Chigmit Mountains	06/30/2008	09/30/2009	Many non-natural spikes in SD data.
Chigmit Mountains	10/01/2008	09/30/2009	Only liquid (e.g. rain) precipitation recorded
Contact Creek	10/01/2008	04/01/2009	Few non-natural spikes in SD data.
Contact Creek	10/01/2008	09/30/2009	Only liquid (e.g. rain) precipitation recorded
Coville	10/01/2008	09/30/2009	Only liquid (e.g. rain) precipitation recorded
Fourpeaked	10/01/2008	06/09/2009	Station not in operation yet
Fourpeaked	06/09/2009	09/30/2009	Little precipitation recorded
Fourpeaked	08/15/2009	09/30/2009	Few non-natural spikes in SD data
Fourpeaked	10/01/2008	09/30/2009	Only liquid (e.g. rain) precipitation recorded
Harding Icefield	10/01/2008	09/30/2009	Significant precipitation undercatch
Harding Icefield	11/25/2008	02/25/2009	Batteries not fully charging
Harding Icefield	10/01/2008	09/30/2009	SD sensor not working
Harding Icefield	01/16/2009	06/03/2009	Mast broken – no WD or WS
Hickerson Lake	11/15/2008	09/30/2009	Few non-natural spikes in SD data
Hickerson Lake	05/07/2008	06/29/2009	Bear damage – no WD or WS
Hickerson Lake	10/01/2008	09/30/2009	Only liquid (e.g. rain) precipitation recorded
McArthur Pass	10/01/2008	09/30/2009	High precipitation recorded during strong wind events
McArthur Pass	10/01/2008	09/30/2009	Only liquid (e.g. rain) precipitation recorded
McArthur Pass	10/01/2008	10/31/2008	Bear damage – no WD
McArthur Pass	10/01/2008	09/30/2009	SD sensor not working
McArthur Pass	01/23/2009	06/02/2009	RH sensor not working
McArthur Pass	03/25/2009	06/02/2009	Mast broken – no WD or WS
Pfaff Mine	10/01/2008	09/30/2009	Few non-natural spikes in SD data
Pfaff Mine	07/04/2009	09/30/2009	RH sensor not working
Pfaff Mine	10/01/2008	09/30/2009	Only liquid (e.g. rain) precipitation recorded
Snipe Lake	07/16/2009	09/30/2009	Bear damage – batteries not charging and no ST
Snipe Lake	05/28/2009	06/27/2009	RH sensor not working
Snipe Lake	10/01/2008	09/30/2009	Few non-natural spikes in SD data
Snipe Lake	10/01/2008	09/30/2009	Only liquid (e.g. rain) precipitation recorded

The SWAN benefits greatly from, and in turn, supports park-based weather and climate monitoring efforts. The Telaquana Lake weather station in LACL was upgraded with a Cotton Region Shelter and accurate liquid-in-glass maximum and minimum thermometers. Efforts are in place to continue to upgrade this weather station and formally include it in the NWS COOP. With support from LACL and SWAN, NOAA installed a CRN station at Port Alsworth in September 2009. The primary goal of the CRN is to collect three independent measurements of temperature and precipitation at each station, insuring a continuous record of well-calibrated and very precise observations that can be coupled to historic observations. KEFJ plans to install a SNOTEL station at Exit Glacier. This automated station would provide continuous weather observations throughout the year, including times when observations are not currently made at the existing COOP station because of staffing or access issues. A new SNOTEL site would provide continuous and accurate precipitation observations including winter-time snowfall, snow depth, and snow water equivalent.

Conclusion

The SWAN region was colder and drier than average during the 2009 hydrologic year (October 2008 through September 2009). Compared to the climatological normal (the prevailing set of weather conditions calculated over a 30-year period, currently 1971-2000), annual mean temperatures for six long-term weather stations were -2.6 to +0.1 °F of normal. Total annual precipitation was 59 to 100% of normal. In general, precipitation across the Alaska Peninsula (western part of the region) was closer to average than precipitation across the Kenai Peninsula (eastern part). These colder and drier than average conditions are consistent with regional climatic conditions for the previous three years.

Literature Cited

Alaska Climate Research Center. 2009. Temperature change in Alaska: Total change in mean seasonal and annual temperature °F, 1949-2008. Available at http://climate.gi.alaska.edu/ClimTrends/Change/TempChange.html (accessed 16 November 2009).

Bennett, A.J., W.L. Thompson, and D.C. Mortenson. 2006. Vital signs monitoring plan, Southwest Alaska Network. National Park Service, Anchorage, Alaska.

Carlisle, J, and K. Nelson, 2009. Redoubt Volcano eruption / ash synopsis – November 2008 – July 2009. Available from http://www.avo.alaska.edu/volcanoes/volcbib.php?volcname=Redoubt (accessed 15 May 2010).

Davey, C.A., K.T. Redmond, and D.B. Simeral. 2007. Weather and climate inventory, National Park Service, Southwest Alaska Network. Natural Resource Technical Report NPS/SWAN/NRTR-2007/045. National Park Service, Fort Collins, Colorado.

Hartman, B., and G. Wendler. 2005. The significance of the 1976 Pacific climate shift in the climatology of Alaska. *Journal of Climate* 18:4824-4839.

Joint Institute for the Study of the Atmosphere and Ocean (JISAO), 2010. Monthly standardized values for the PDO index. Available at http://jisao.washington.edu/pdo/PDO.latest (accessed 13, May 2010).

National Climatic Data Center, 2010. Global Historical Climatology Network – Daily: Methods – quality control. Available at http://www.ncdc.noaa.gov/oa/climate/ghcn-daily/ (accessed 10 May 2010).

National Park Service, 2010. Landscape processes vital signs monitoring. Southwest Alaska Network Inventory and Monitoring Program Unpublished Data, Anchorage, Alaska.

National Weather Service (NWS) Climate Prediction Center, 2010. Previous ENSO events 1951-present. Available at http://www.cpc.ncep.noaa.gov/products/analysis_monitoring/ensostuff/ensoyears.shtml (accessed 10 May 2010).

Natural Resources Conservation Service (NRCS), 2009. Alaska Snow Survey Reports. Natural Resources Conservation Service, Anchorage, Alaska.

Papineau, J. 2004. A fresh look at persistent ridging in the North Pacific. American Meteorological Society 20th Conference on Weather Analysis and Forecasting/16th Conference on Numerical Weather Prediction. Seattle, Washington.

Papineau, J. 2005. Winter temperature variability across Alaska during El Niño events. Alaska Region Research Notes RN-05-0002. National Weather Service, Anchorage, Alaska.

Papineau, J., no date. Understanding Alaska's climate variation. Available from
http://pafc.arh.noaa.gov/climvar/climate-paper.html (accessed 14 May 2010).

PRISM Climate Group, Oregon State University and Alaska Region Inventory and Monitoring
Program, National Park Service, 2010. Gridded temperature and precipitation data for Alaska
for the 1971-2000 climatological normal. Available from
http://science.nature.nps.gov/nrdata/ (accessed and manipulated 4 April, 2010).

Redmond, K.T., D.B. Simeral, and G.D. McCurdy. 2005. Climate monitoring for southwest
Alaska national parks: Network design and site selection. Western Regional Climate Center,
Reno, Nevada.

Scenarios Network for Alaska Planning. 2008. Climate change summary reports: Aniakchak
National Monument and Preserve, Katmai National Park and Preserve, Kenai Fjords National
Park and Preserve, and Lake Clark National Park and Preserve. Available from
http://www.snap.uaf.edu/downloads/climate-change-summary-reports (accessed 15
November 2009).

Simpson, J.J., G.L. Hufford, M.D. Fleming, J.S. Berg, and J. Ashton. 2002. Long-term climate
patterns in Alaskan surface temperature and precipitation and their biological consequences.
IEEE Transactions on Geoscience and Remote Sensing 40:1164-1184.

Shearer, J., and C. Moore. 2010. Water quality and surface hydrology of freshwater flow systems
in southwest Alaska: 2009 annual summary report. Natural Resource Technical Report
NPS/SWAN/NRTR-2010/304. National Park Service, Fort Collins, Colorado.

Spencer, P., A.E. Miller, B. Reed, and M. Budde. 2008. Monitoring lake ice seasons in southwest
Alaska with MODIS images. Proceedings of Pecora 17 Conference. Denver, Colorado.

Weller, G. P. Anderson, and B. Wang, eds. 1999. Preparing for a changing climate: The potential
consequences of climate change and variability in Alaska. Alaska Regional Assessment
Group Report, U.S. Global Change Research Program. Fairbanks, Alaska.

Appendices

Summary reports and graphs for the most consistently measured climate variables from all weather stations monitored by the SWAN are included in the appendices and are organized by park, climate monitoring program, and station name. Daily measures are used for generating graphs (with the exception of NRCS Snow Courses) and monthly measures are used for generating summary reports. Mean temperature, total precipitation, mean snow depth, mean wind speed and direction, and maximum wind speed are presented in graphs. Minimum, maximum, and mean temperature data, the number of frost days (number of days where the minimum temperature is below freezing), and the number of ice days (number of days where the maximum temperature is below freezing) are included in the summary reports. Total precipitation, average snow depth, mean and maximum wind speed, maximum wind direction, and cumulative solar radiation are also presented in the summary reports. The percentage of valid observations is reported as a measure of the reliability of the derived mean and cumulative values for all reported climate variables. Climatic normal values (arithmetic mean over a 30-year interval) from the NCDC for the 1971-2000 period and period of record (POR) values from the WRCC are included for stations with a long enough observational record.

For all derived measures, the percentage of valid observations is reported as a measure of the reliability of the derived mean and cumulative values. Monthly measures should not be considered representative of actual climatic conditions if more than 10% (three days) of observations are missing or suspect. Yearly measures should not be considered representative if more than 17% (five days) are missing from any month.

Data from the Port Alsworth CRN is not included in this report because of the short period of record (only days) during the 2009 hydrologic year.

All data used in this report are available upon request from the SWAN. Station data is available in a standardized format - summarized at hourly (where available), daily, and monthly intervals in both metric and U.S. customary units.

2009 Hydrologic Year – ANIA AWOS POHE (Port Heiden)													
	Oct	Nov	Dec	Jan	Feb	Mar	Apr	May	Jun	Jul	Aug	Sep	Year
Minimum air temperature (°F)													
Min.	17.7	1	-4	-20	-6	-11	10	27.3	32.7	38	37	35.3	-20
Max.	39	36	43	37	30.7	36	43	45	46	55	52	52	55
Mean	30.2	18.9	24.5	12.6	17.3	15.7	27.2	32.5	40.9	46.9	46.5	43.2	29.7
# days < 32 °F	16	27	22	27	28	29	21	14	1	1	0	3	189
% valid obs	89.8	94.3	93.8	87.9	93.5	93.8	87.6	96.9	84.4	85.9	98.3	81.7	90.7
Maximum air temperature (°F)													
Min.	28.7	14	3	-8	7	5	19.7	34	43	48	50	44	-8
Max.	54	40.3	46	44	42.3	57	53	63	63.7	72	63.5	63.7	72
Mean	40.6	29.6	33.1	24	30.6	27.7	37.8	46.5	52.4	57.8	54.9	51.9	40.5
# days < 32 °F	1	17	10	19	11	17	8	0	1	1	0	3	88
% valid obs	89.8	94.3	93.8	87.9	93.5	93.8	87.6	96.9	84.4	85.9	98.3	81.7	90.7
Mean air temperature (°F)													
Observed	35.4	24.8	28.6	18	24.4	21.6	31.7	39.6	47.1	52.8	50.5	47.5	35.1
% valid obs	89.8	94.3	93.8	87.9	93.5	93.8	87.6	96.9	84.4	85.9	98.3	81.7	90.7
POR mean													
1971-2000													
Precipitation (in)													
Total													
% valid obs													
POR mean													
1971-2000													
Snow depth (in)													
Average													
% valid obs													
POR mean													
Wind (mph, degrees)													
Mean speed	11.5	11.3	15.9	13.9	14.7	14.5	15.4	11	12.6	12	12.2	9.7	
% valid obs	90.6	94.4	99.7	90.3	98.7	97.6	97.8	99.1	87.8	88.6	99.2	81.7	
Max speed													
Max direction													
Solar radiation (KWh/m^2)													
Total													
% valid obs													

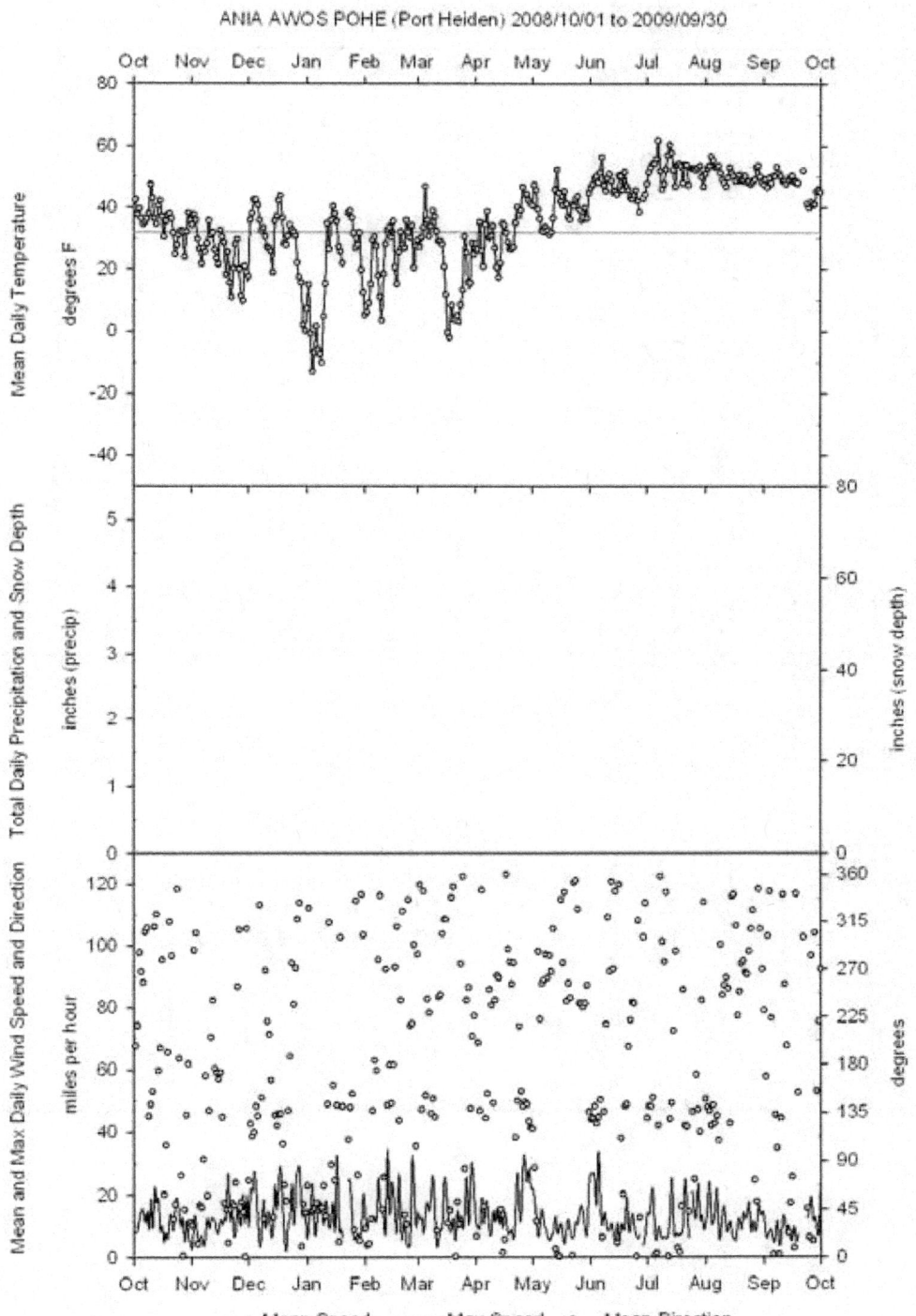

ANIA AWOS POHE (Port Heiden) 2008/10/01 to 2009/09/30

35

2009 Hydrologic Year – KATM ASOS KISA (King Salmon Airport)

	Oct	Nov	Dec	Jan	Feb	Mar	Apr	May	Jun	Jul	Aug	Sep	Year
Minimum air temperature (°F)													
Min.	-1.3	-21	-21	-32	-33	-11	4	25	32.7	36.9	32	25.7	-33
Max.	38	31	38	37	33.3	33	44	45	48	54	53	47	54
Mean	20.4	7.2	15.2	4.5	6.4	11.3	25.5	33.6	40.8	47.2	44.2	38.2	24.7
# days < 32 °F	25	30	25	26	26	29	21	10	0	0	0	5	197
% valid obs	100	100	100	100	100	99.7	100	99.9	100	100	100	100	100
Maximum air temperature (°F)													
Min.	22	-2	-9	-19	-8	-3	22	41	48	52.5	50	42.5	-19
Max.	50	41	45	45	40	44	55	71	81	80	72	69	81
Mean	36.6	22.8	26.7	17.1	25.8	24.4	39	56.9	60.3	65.7	60.7	55.9	41.1
# days < 32 °F	8	22	15	20	16	18	6	0	0	0	0	0	105
% valid obs	100	100	100	100	100	99.7	100	99.9	100	100	100	100	100
Mean air temperature (°F)													
Observed	29	16.2	21.7	11.3	16.6	18.3	32.5	45.8	50.6	56.8	52.6	46.8	33.3
% valid obs	100	100	100	100	100	99.7	100	99.9	100	100	100	100	100
POR mean 1971-2000													
Precipitation (in)													
Total*	2.7	0.74	1.69	1.05	1.23	1.53	0.63	1.1	2.12	2.72	1.68	2.26	19.45
% valid obs	100	100	100	100	100	99.7	100	99.9	100	100	100	100	100
POR mean 1971-2000													
Snow depth (in)													
Average													
% valid obs													
POR mean													
Wind (mph, degrees)													
Mean speed	8	8.1	9.5	9.7	9.1	11.1	11.6	9.4	7.7	8.7	8.2	7.3	
% valid obs	100	100	100	100	100	99.7	100	99.9	100	100	100		
Max speed													
Max direction													
Solar radiation (KWh/m²)													
Total													
% valid obs													

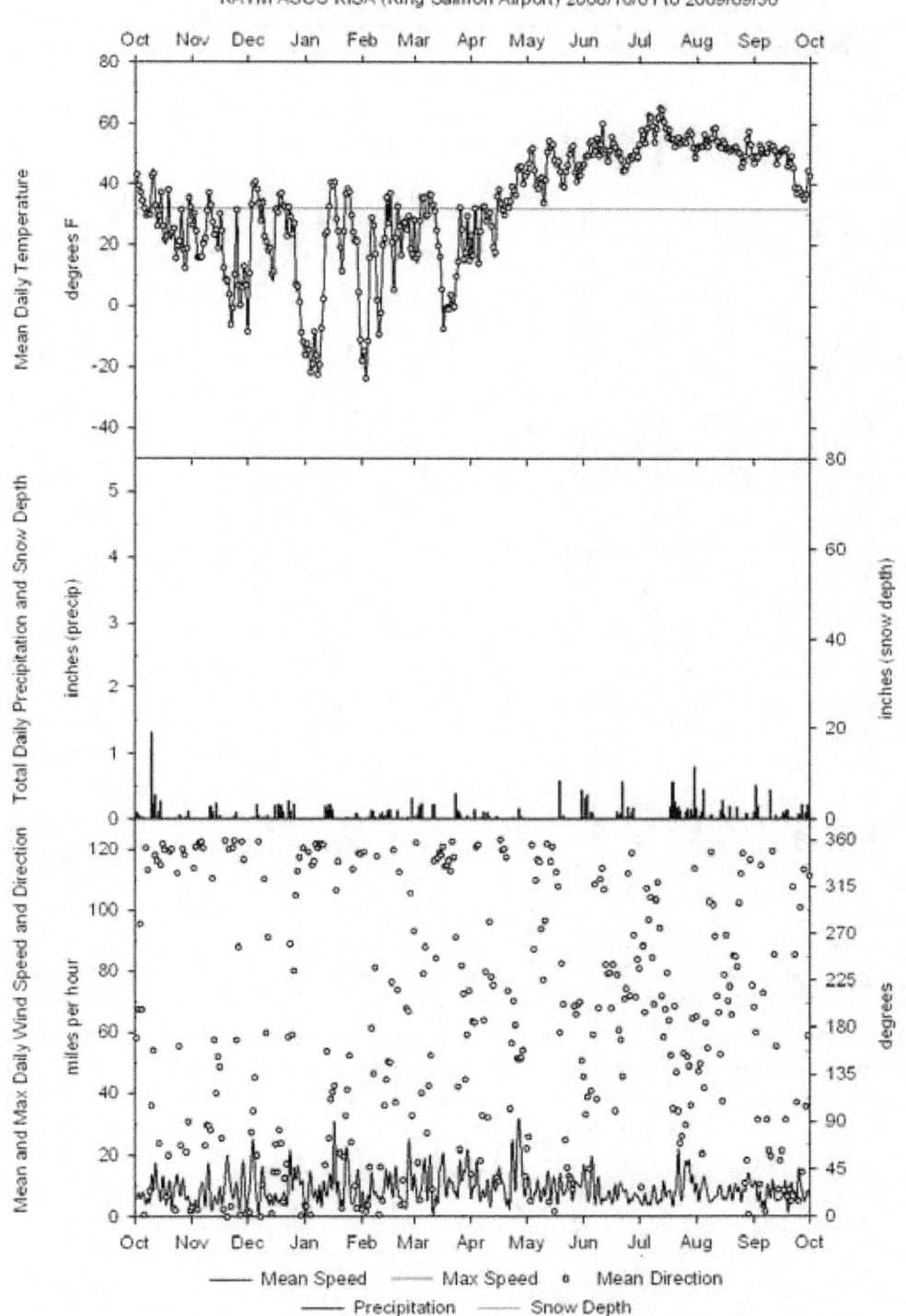

KATM ASOS KISA (King Salmon Airport) 2008/10/01 to 2009/09/30

2009 Hydrologic Year – KATM BUOY SHST (Shelikof Strait)	Oct	Nov	Dec	Jan	Feb	Mar	Apr	May	Jun	Jul	Aug	Sep	Year
Minimum air temperature (°F)													
Min.	27.7	24.6	17.8	9	14	12.2	25.5	36.9	39.9	47.7	49.3	41.9	9
Max.	47.5	40.3	41	40.6	34.5	36.7	40.8	45.1	49.1	53.1	53.1	52	53.1
Mean	38.8	33.5	32.9	28.6	27.7	26.4	34.5	41.4	45.5	50.7	51.4	48.2	38.4
# days < 32 °F	2	8	8	16	20	23	7	0	0	0	0	0	84
% valid obs	99.5	100	99.9	100	99.6	100	100	100	100	100	99.6	99.7	99.9
Maximum air temperature (°F)													
Min.	37.2	27.9	22.5	20.5	23.9	25.7	30.4	40.6	42.8	51.1	50.9	45.3	20.5
Max.	50.4	42.4	43.3	46.6	39	39	46	48.9	56.1	56.3	57.7	56.5	57.7
Mean	43.7	38.3	37	34	33.6	33.1	38.5	45.1	48.5	53.6	54.5	51.5	42.7
# days < 32 °F	0	2	5	12	9	12	1	0	0	0	0	0	41
% valid obs	99.5	100	99.9	100	99.6	100	100	100	100	100	99.6	99.7	99.9
Mean air temperature (°F)													
Observed	41.1	35.7	34.9	31.3	30.5	29.5	36.6	42.9	46.7	51.9	52.6	49.6	40.3
% valid obs	99.5	100	99.9	100	99.6	100	100	100	100	100	99.6	99.7	99.9
POR mean													
1971-2000													
Precipitation (in)													
Total													
% valid obs													
POR mean													
1971-2000													
Snow depth (in)													
Average													
% valid obs													
POR mean													
Wind (mph, degrees)													
Mean speed	14.7												
% valid obs	99.3	0	0	0	0	0	0	0	0	0	0	0	
Max speed													
Max direction													
Solar radiation (KWh/m^2)													
Total													
% valid obs													

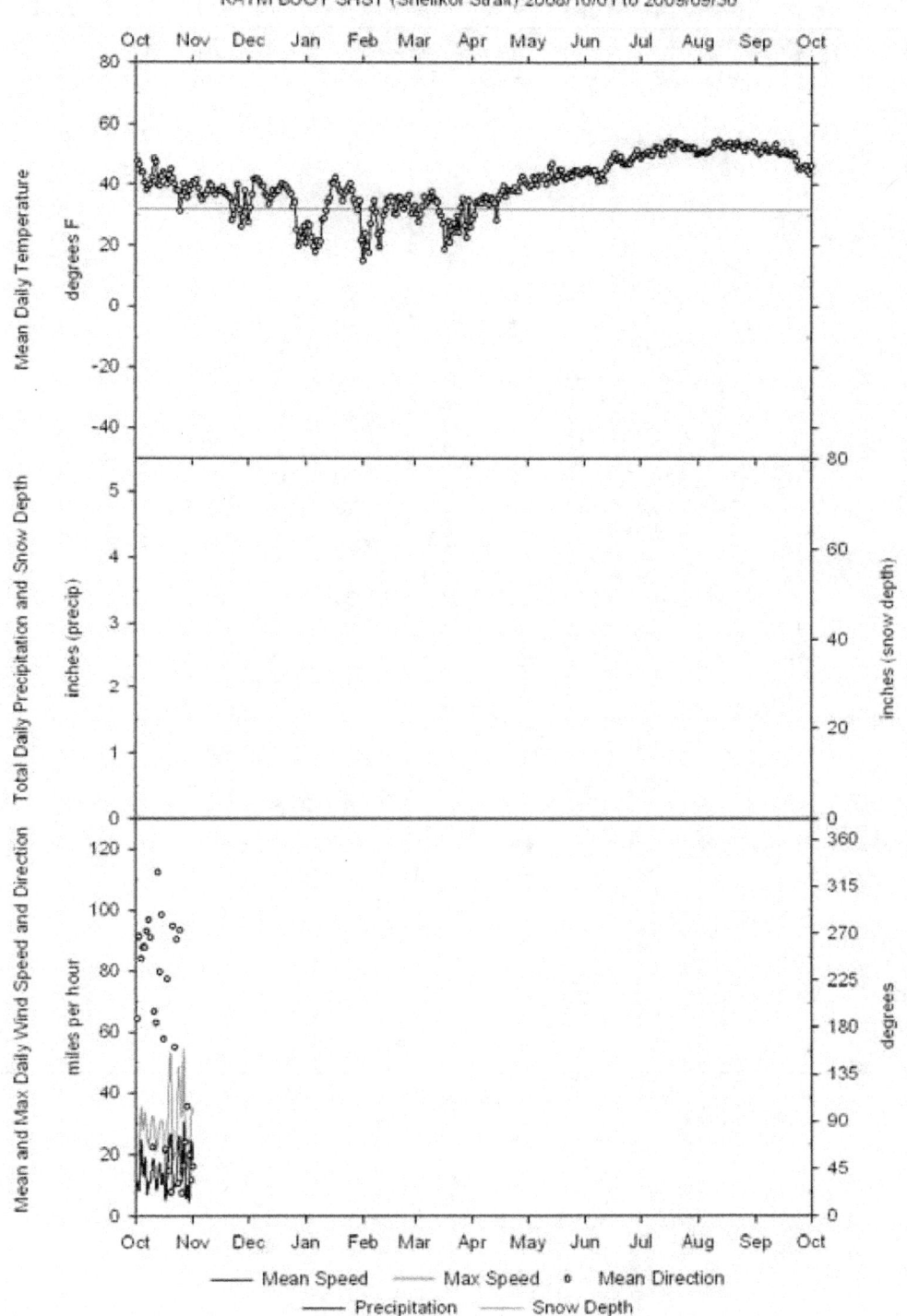

KATM BUOY SHST (Shelikof Strait) 2008/10/01 to 2009/09/30

2009 Hydrologic Year – KATM COOP KISA (King Salmon Airport)

	Oct	Nov	Dec	Jan	Feb	Mar	Apr	May	Jun	Jul	Aug	Sep	Year
Minimum air temperature (°F)													
Min.	-3	-21	-21	-33	-34	-12	2	24	32	36	30	25	-34
Max.	38	31	37	37	32	33	44	45	48	54	53	47	54
Mean	19.7	6.4	14.4	3.7	5.4	11	25	33.2	39.9	46.6	43.7	37.6	24
# days < 32 °F	26	30	25	26	26	29	21	12	0	0	1	5	201
% valid obs	100	100	100	100	100	100	100	100	100	100	100	100	100
Maximum air temperature (°F)													
Min.	23	-2	-9	-17	-7	-3	22	41	48	53	50	42	-17
Max.	52	42	45	46	41	44	56	73	81	80	73	69	81
Mean	37.3	23.2	27	17.7	26.5	24.7	39.4	57.8	61.2	66.7	61.3	56.6	41.7
# days < 32 °F	8	21	15	20	14	17	6	0	0	0	0	0	101
% valid obs	100	100	100	100	100	100	100	100	100	100	100	100	100
Mean air temperature (°F)													
Observed	28.6	14.8	20.8	10.7	16	18.1	32.3	45.5	50.5	56.7	52.4	47.1	32.9
% valid obs	100	100	100	100	100	100	100	100	100	100	100	100	100
POR mean[1]	33.2	22.7	15.7	14.8	17.0	22.2	32.6	43.3	50.8	55.1	54.3	47.3	34.1
1971-2000	33.3	23.2	17.2	15.4	15.6	23.5	33.1	43.5	50.9	55.7	54.8	47.6	34.5
Precipitation (in)													
Total	2.7	0.74	1.7	1.06	1.23	1.52	0.64	1.1	2.12	2.72	1.68	2.26	19.48
% valid obs	100	100	100	100	100	100	100	100	100	100	100	100	100
POR mean[1]	2.09	1.46	1.25	1.01	0.77	0.89	1.01	1.30	1.60	2.25	2.99	3.04	19.66
1971-2000	2.10	1.54	1.39	1.03	0.72	0.79	0.94	1.35	1.70	2.15	2.89	2.81	19.41
Snow depth (in)													
Average	0	3	2	3	5	3	2	0	0	0	0	0	
% valid obs	100	100	100	100	100	100	100	100	100	100	100	100	
POR mean[1]	0	1	2	3	3	2	1	0	0	0	0	0	
Wind (mph, degrees)													
Mean speed													
% valid obs													
Max speed													
Max direction													
Solar radiation (KWh/m^2)													
Total													
% valid obs													

[1]Period of record used: 7/01/1955 to 12/31/2009

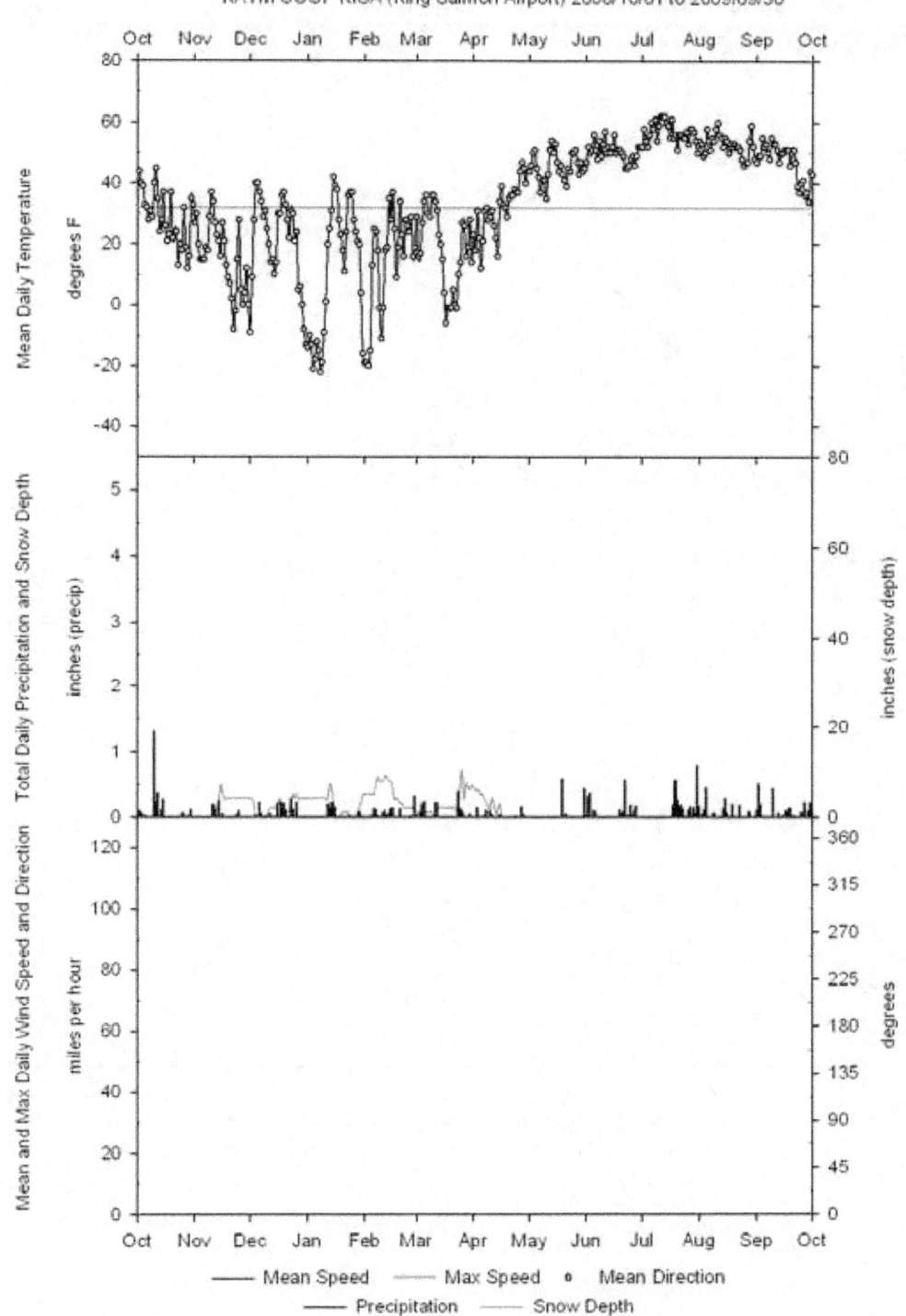

KATM COOP KISA (King Salmon Airport) 2008/10/01 to 2009/09/30

2009 Hydrologic Year – KATM RAWS COCR (Contact Creek)													
	Oct	Nov	Dec	Jan	Feb	Mar	Apr	May	Jun	Jul	Aug	Sep	Year
Minimum air temperature (°F)													
Min.	0.3	-14.3	-27.2	-32.6	-26	-18.6	-1.1	21.2	30.6	32.7	28.9	24.1	-32.6
Max.	36.5	33.3	37.2	36.5	31.3	32.2	39	41.9	45.5	52.7	52.7	47.1	52.7
Mean	20.5	8.3	15.5	5.8	7.6	8.2	24.1	31.0	38.4	45.3	42.5	36.0	23.7
# days < 32 °F	27	29	25	25	28	30	21	19	1	0	2	7	214
% valid obs	100	100	100	100	100	100	100	100	99.9	98.7	100	100	99.9
Maximum air temperature (°F)													
Min.	27.7	4.1	-7.8	-17.3	-0.9	0	23.2	43.3	49.8	52	49.5	41.2	-17.3
Max.	52.2	43.9	44.1	48.7	37.4	48.2	52.5	70.2	75.7	79.3	71.2	68.5	79.3
Mean	38.7	25.8	28.8	21	28.1	26.5	41.1	56.8	59.1	64.2	59.5	54.4	42.1
# days < 32 °F	5	20	12	17	13	17	3	0	0	0	0	0	87
% valid obs	100	100	100	100	100	100	100	100	99.9	98.8	100	100	99.9
Mean air temperature (°F)													
Observed	29.8	17.5	22.9	13.1	18.2	17.4	32.2	44.6	48.7	54.8	51	45.5	33
% valid obs	100	100	100	100	100	100	100	100	99.9	98.9	100	100	99.9
POR mean 1971-2000													
Precipitation (in)													
Total[2]	2.58	0.58	0.87	1.26	0.69	0.65	0.33	1.29	2.03	2.09	2.29	1.81	16.47
% valid obs	52.3	19.6	43.8	34.7	23.1	27.4	65.7	93.7	99.7	98.8	99.9	96.9	63.2
POR mean 1971-2000													
Snow depth (in)													
Average	0.3	2.8	2.2	2.6	2.4	2.9	5.4	0.4	0.2	0.1	0.1	0.1	
% valid obs	55.1	99.7	99.9	99.2	100	99.9	100	68.1	52.8	11.3	31	37.4	
POR mean													
Wind (mph, degrees)													
Mean speed	8.5	7.2	11.6	9.8	11.9	11.5	12.5	9.8	10.5	11.7	10.1	7.5	
% valid obs	100	100	100	100	100	100	100	100	99.9	98.9	100	100	
Max speed	43.2	46.5	53	75.4	60.4	51.5	47.2	39.6	43.2	47.9	39.4	32.2	75.4
Max direction	331	344	92	122	106	108	128	37	120	76	110	350	122
Solar radiation (KWh/m²)													
Total	46.4	20.1	9.6	17.7	38.1	88.5	123.7	178.4	161.9	151.2	108.8	72.6	1017
% valid obs	100	100	100	100	100	100	100	100	99.9	98.9	100	100	99.9

[2]Station is only capable of measuring liquid precipitation. Precipitation reported when maximum air temperature is below 31.1 °F is not considered valid and these data are not used for summarizing purposes. The water equivalent of solid precipitation (e.g. snowfall) is not measured and this is reflected in the percentage of valid observations that are reported as a measure of the reliability of cumulative values.

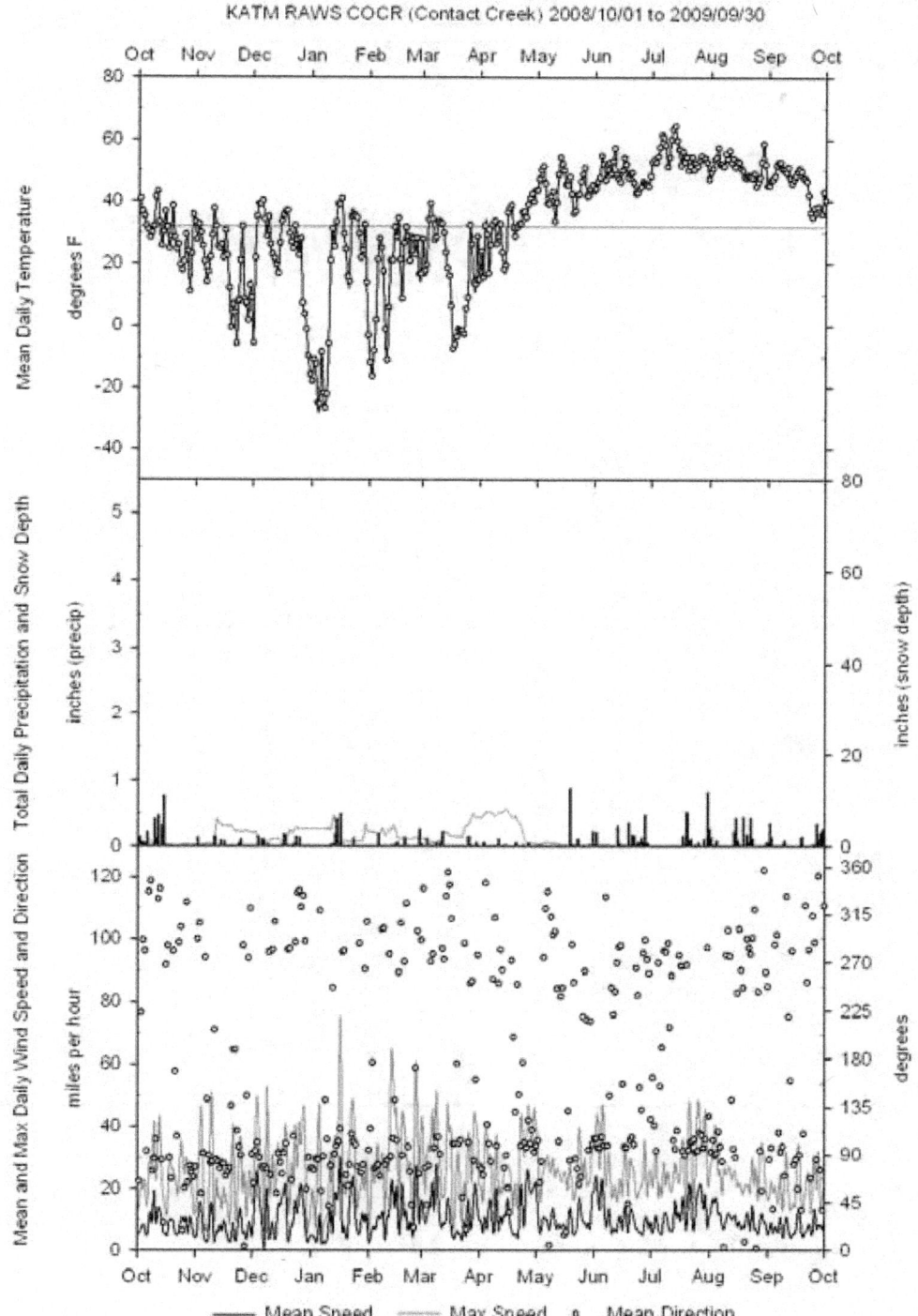

KATM RAWS COCR (Contact Creek) 2008/10/01 to 2009/09/30

43

2009 Hydrologic Year – KATM RAWS COVI (Coville)	Oct	Nov	Dec	Jan	Feb	Mar	Apr	May	Jun	Jul	Aug	Sep	Year
Minimum air temperature (°F)													
Min.	2.1	-14.3	-17.1	-27	-16.2	-20.6	1.9	24.8	32	40.3	35.4	28	-27
Max.	37.8	30.7	37.2	36.3	31.8	30.2	40.5	45	50.2	56.3	52.7	46.8	56.3
Mean	21.4	10.9	17.2	8.9	10.4	7.6	23.7	34.8	41.1	48.3	43.8	38.7	25.7
# days < 32 °F	29	30	25	27	28	31	23	10	0	0	0	7	210
% valid obs	100	100	100	100	100	100	100	100	99.9	99.7	100	97.9	99.8
Maximum air temperature (°F)													
Min.	15.3	2.7	-5.4	-9.4	-7.8	-8	21.4	37.8	47.1	48.7	44.4	34.3	-9.4
Max.	46	36.7	41	47.7	42.1	50.2	50.9	65.1	73.9	78.8	67.1	65.5	78.8
Mean	32.8	24	26.4	21.2	26.3	22.7	37	51.9	56.6	63.6	56.8	50.9	39.3
# days < 32 °F	12	22	17	20	17	21	8	0	0	0	0	0	117
% valid obs	100	100	100	100	100	100	100	100	99.9	99.7	100	97.9	99.8
Mean air temperature (°F)													
Observed	27	17.8	22	15	17.9	14.7	30.2	43.4	48.1	55.4	49.6	44.4	32.2
% valid obs	100	100	100	100	100	100	100	100	99.9	99.7	100	97.9	99.8
POR mean 1971-2000													
Precipitation (in)													
Total[2]	3.48	0	0.42	0.61	0.66	0.97	0.3	1.18	3.16	3.66	3.15	2.75	20.34
% valid obs	37.1	11.7	31.7	27	14.4	18.1	52.9	94.2	99.7	99.6	100	93.2	56.9
POR mean 1971-2000													
Snow depth (in)													
Average	1.4	2.7	3.6	4.2	2.3	3.5	5.1	0.4					
% valid obs	85.3	100	99.3	98.8	99.9	100	100	47.2					
POR mean													
Wind (mph, degrees)													
Mean speed	9	7.9	11	10.2	10.8	12.3	11.3	10.9	8.7	10.5	9.2	9.5	
% valid obs	100	100	100	100	100	100	100	100	99.9	99.7	100	97.9	
Max speed	48.3	70.5	72.7	81.7	71.1	67.3	47.7	38.9	37.8	70.5	37.6	42.5	81.7
Max direction	117	82	101	82	221	94	126	68	121	102	86	75	82
Solar radiation (KWh/m²)													
Total	46.4	20.1	9.6	17.7	38.1	88.5	123.7	178.4	161.9	151.2	108.8	72.6	950
% valid obs	100	100	100	100	100	100	100	100	99.9	98.9	100	100	99.8

[2]Station is only capable of measuring liquid precipitation. Precipitation reported when maximum air temperature is below 31.1 °F is not considered valid and these data are not used for summarizing purposes. The water equivalent of solid precipitation (e.g. snowfall) is not measured and this is reflected in the percentage of valid observations that are reported as a measure of the reliability of cumulative values.

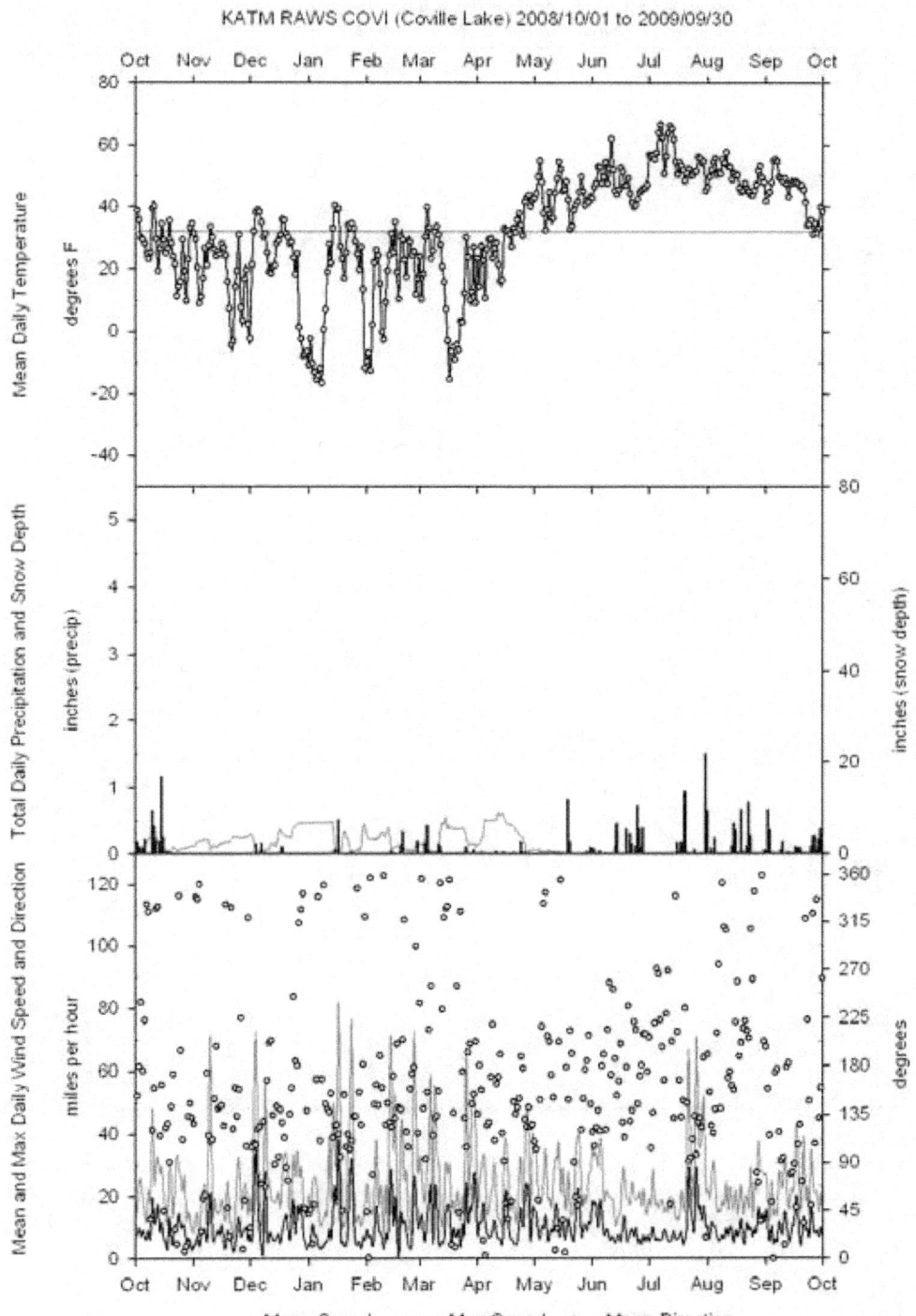

KATM RAWS COVI (Coville Lake) 2008/10/01 to 2009/09/30

2009 Hydrologic Year – KATM RAWS FOUR (Fourpeaked)												
	Oct	Nov	Dec	Jan	Feb	Mar	Apr	May	Jun	Jul	Aug	Sep	Year
Minimum air temperature (°F)												
Min.									38.1	43	43	35.1	35.1
Max.									51.8	62.6	59.2	54.5	62.6
Mean									42.9	49.1	48.3	43	46.2
# days < 32 °F									0	0	0	0	0
% valid obs									65.6	99.6	100	99.9	30.5
Maximum air temperature (°F)												
Min.									43.7	46.4	47.8	39.7	39.7
Max.									61.7	73.8	68.5	66.6	73.8
Mean									0	0	0	0	0
# days < 32 °F												
% valid obs												
Mean air temperature (°F)												
Observed									46.9	53.4	52.3	46.4	50.1
% valid obs									65.6	99.6	100	99.9	30.5
POR mean												
1971-2000												
Precipitation (in)												
Total[2]									0	0.07	0.09	0.07	0.23
% valid obs									65.6	96.6	99.7	96	30
POR mean												
1971-2000												
Snow depth (in)												
Average									0.6	0.4	0.3	0.4	
% valid obs									65.6	81	86.3	81.7	
POR mean												
Wind (mph, degrees)												
Mean speed									10.9	13.2	10.9	18.2	
% valid obs									65.6	99.6	100	99.9	
Max speed									59.7	100.9	70.9	86.6	100.9
Max direction									303	64	38	72	64
Solar radiation (KWh/m^2)												
Total									105.4	144.4	131.4	56.2	437.4
% valid obs									62.5	99.6	100	99.9	30.3

[2]Station is only capable of measuring liquid precipitation. Precipitation reported when maximum air temperature is below 31.1 °F is not considered valid and these data are not used for summarizing purposes. The water equivalent of solid precipitation (e.g. snowfall) is not measured and this is reflected in the percentage of valid observations that are reported as a measure of the reliability of cumulative values.

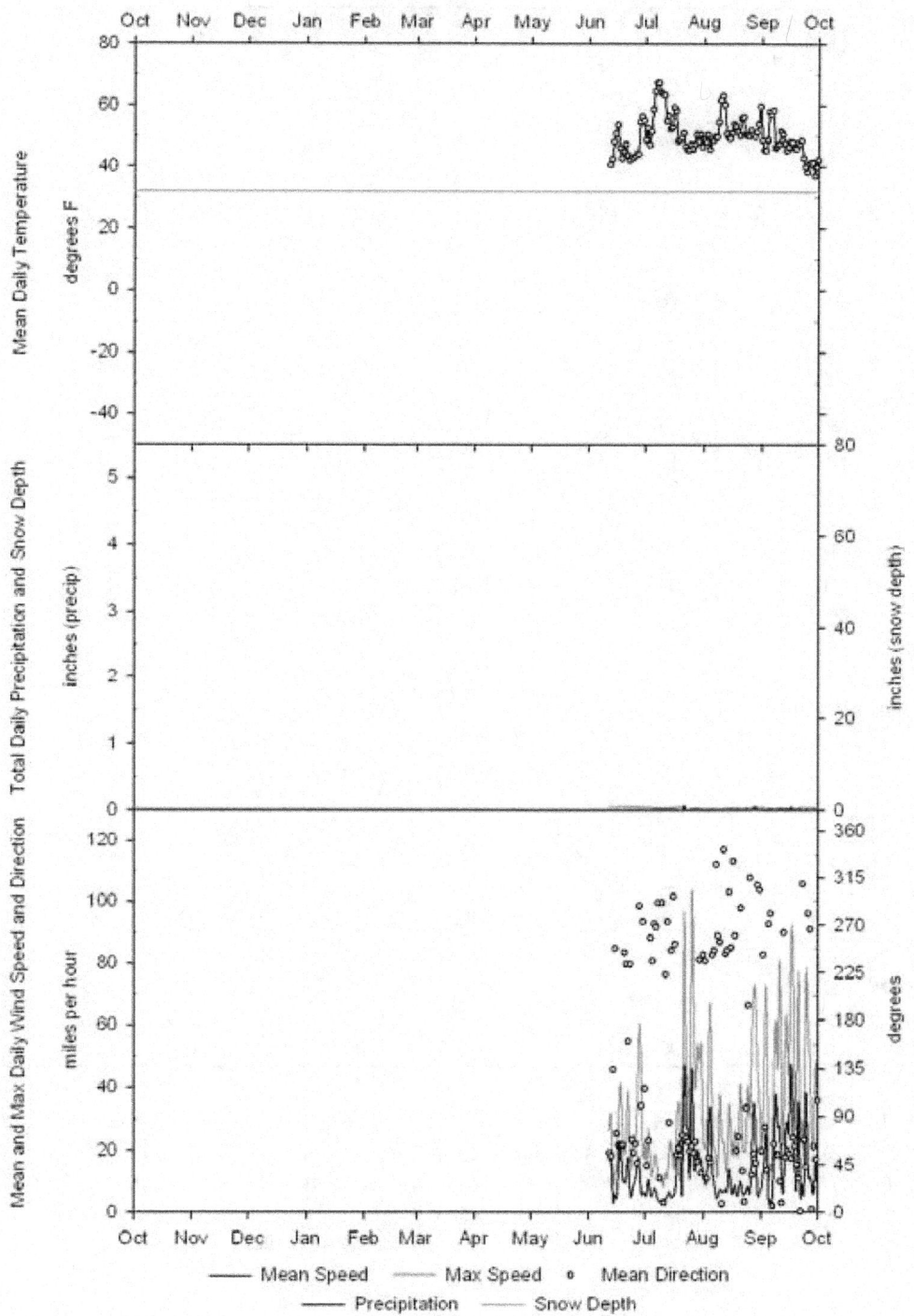

2009 Hydrologic Year – KATM RAWS PFMI (Pfaff Mine)

	Oct	Nov	Dec	Jan	Feb	Mar	Apr	May	Jun	Jul	Aug	Sep	Year
Minimum air temperature (°F)													
Min.	3.7	-13.9	-15.9	-26	-17.3	-21.1	2.7	25.9	32	40.6	36.3	26.2	-26
Max.	34	27	32	32.2	26.8	26.8	37.6	44.4	48	57.2	48.9	49.6	57.2
Mean	20.1	11.3	14.7	7.3	9.3	6	22.6	35.3	39.5	47.3	43.9	38.8	24.8
# days < 32 °F	29	30	30	30	28	31	27	10	0	0	0	8	223
% valid obs	100	100	100	100	100	100	100	100	99.9	99.9	100	100	100
Maximum air temperature (°F)													
Min.	15.8	5.7	-6.7	-11.7	-10.1	-9.9	20.1	33.3	43.3	46.4	47.8	32.2	-11.7
Max.	43.9	32.7	37	41.9	42.1	36.7	48.6	59.9	66.7	78.1	66.7	65.7	78.1
Mean	30.9	22.7	23.9	19.4	23.7	20.6	36.5	49.1	53.4	61.2	55.7	47.8	37.1
# days < 32 °F	17	29	24	26	24	26	11	0	0	0	0	0	157
% valid obs	100	100	100	100	100	100	100	100	99.9	99.9	100	100	100
Mean air temperature (°F)													
Observed	25.3	17.2	19.4	13.4	16	13.1	28.8	42.1	46.1	53.9	48.9	42.7	30.7
% valid obs	100	100	100	100	100	100	100	100	99.9	99.9	100	100	100
POR mean 1971-2000													
Precipitation (in)													
Total[2]	1.18	0	0.01	0.4	0.12	0.02	0.04	0.97	0.86	3.71	1.16	7.2	15.67
% valid obs	25.5	1	15.2	11	3.3	5.1	44.3	94.6	99.7	97.4	100	92.2	49.4
POR mean 1971-2000													
Snow depth (in)													
Average	2.2	2.3	2.1	2.2	2	3.6	2.7	0.2	0				
% valid obs	86.2	99.2	95.6	92.7	98.7	96.9	85.3	2.2	30.8				
POR mean													
Wind (mph, degrees)													
Mean speed	11.3	11.9	19.3	17.8	15	17.3	14.6	9.2	10.8	12.6	11	11.4	
% valid obs	100	100	100	100	100	100	100	100	99.9	99.9	100	100	
Max speed	78.7	74	96.2	90.8	102	97.8	73.6	54.8	62	84.3	64.4	69.1	102
Max direction	116	107	118	124	133	117	122	144	114	137	112	79	133
Solar radiation (KWh/m^2)													
Total	36.9	17.3	7.3	14.1	32.3	78.1	133.3	185.8	162.6	156.4	108	60.5	992.6
% valid obs	100	100	100	100	100	100	100	100	99.9	99.9	100	100	100

[2]Station is only capable of measuring liquid precipitation. Precipitation reported when maximum air temperature is below 31.1 °F is not considered valid and these data are not used for summarizing purposes. The water equivalent of solid precipitation (e.g. snowfall) is not measured and this is reflected in the percentage of valid observations that are reported as a measure of the reliability of cumulative values.

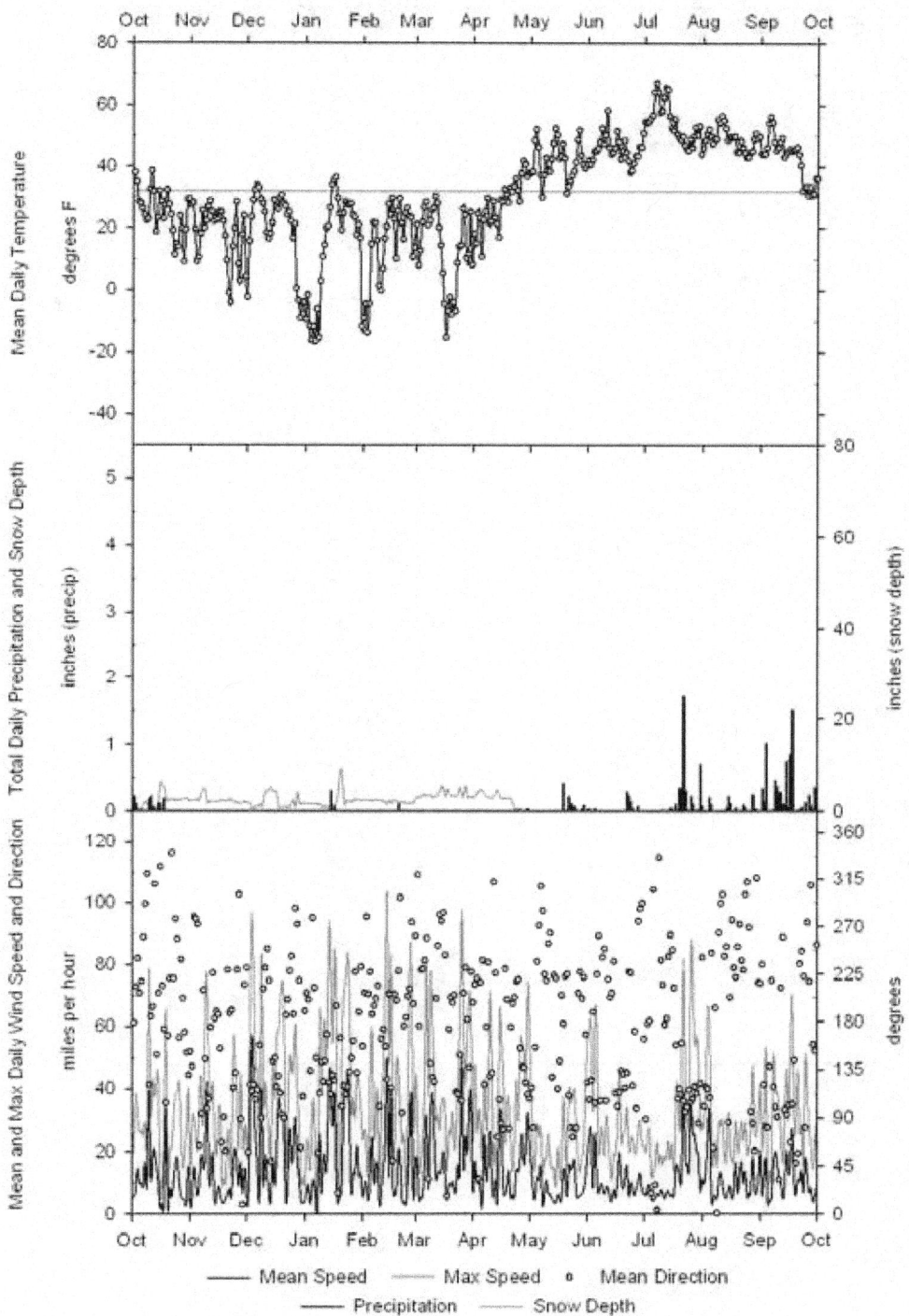

KATM RAWS PFMI (Pfaff Mine) 2008/10/01 to 2009/09/30

2009 Hydrologic Year – KEFJ ASOS HOAI (Homer Airport)													
	Oct	Nov	Dec	Jan	Feb	Mar	Apr	May	Jun	Jul	Aug	Sep	Year
Minimum air temperature (°F)													
Min.	15	10	-4	-8	-7	3	17	30	37	42	39	28	-8
Max.	39	36	35	41	35	36	43	45.5	47	54	54	50	54
Mean	28.4	21.8	18.6	15	15.7	20.8	29.9	36.5	42	48.8	46.4	41.8	30.6
# days < 32 °F	23	26	26	23	26	26	22	1	0	0	0	1	174
% valid obs	100	99.9	100	98.8	100	99.7	100	100	100	99.9	100	100	99.9
Maximum air temperature (°F)													
Min.	30	22	9	2	9	18	29	43	50	55	52	44	2
Max.	51	41	43	46	39	40	54	65	71	66	65	62	71
Mean	40.6	32.5	29	26.1	28.9	32	42.3	52.2	56.6	60.3	59.3	53.9	42.9
# days < 32 °F	1	11	19	18	14	13	1	0	0	0	0	0	77
% valid obs	100	99.9	100	98.8	100	99.7	100	100	100	99.9	100	100	99.9
Mean air temperature (°F)													
Observed	34.8	27.4	24.2	20.5	22.5	26.6	36.7	45.2	49.9	55.3	53.1	48.2	37.1
% valid obs	100	99.9	100	98.8	100	99.7	100	100	100	99.9	100	100	99.9
POR mean													
1971-2000													
Precipitation (in)													
Total	2.25	1.71	1.15	1.44	0.69	0.67	0.31	0.83	0.4	0.94	2.05	2.46	14.9
% valid obs	100	99.9	100	98.8	100	99.7	100	100	100	99.9	100	100	99.9
POR mean													
1971-2000													
Snow depth (in)													
Average													
% valid obs													
POR mean													
Wind (mph, degrees)													
Mean speed	5.5	6.1	4.8	5.7	4.8	6.9	5.7	5.8	5.9	5.8	5	4.9	
% valid obs	98.8	99.9	99.9	98.7	99	98.1	100	100	100	99.9	100	99.9	
Max speed													
Max direction													
Solar radiation (KWh/m^2)													
Total													
% valid obs													

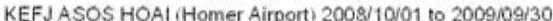

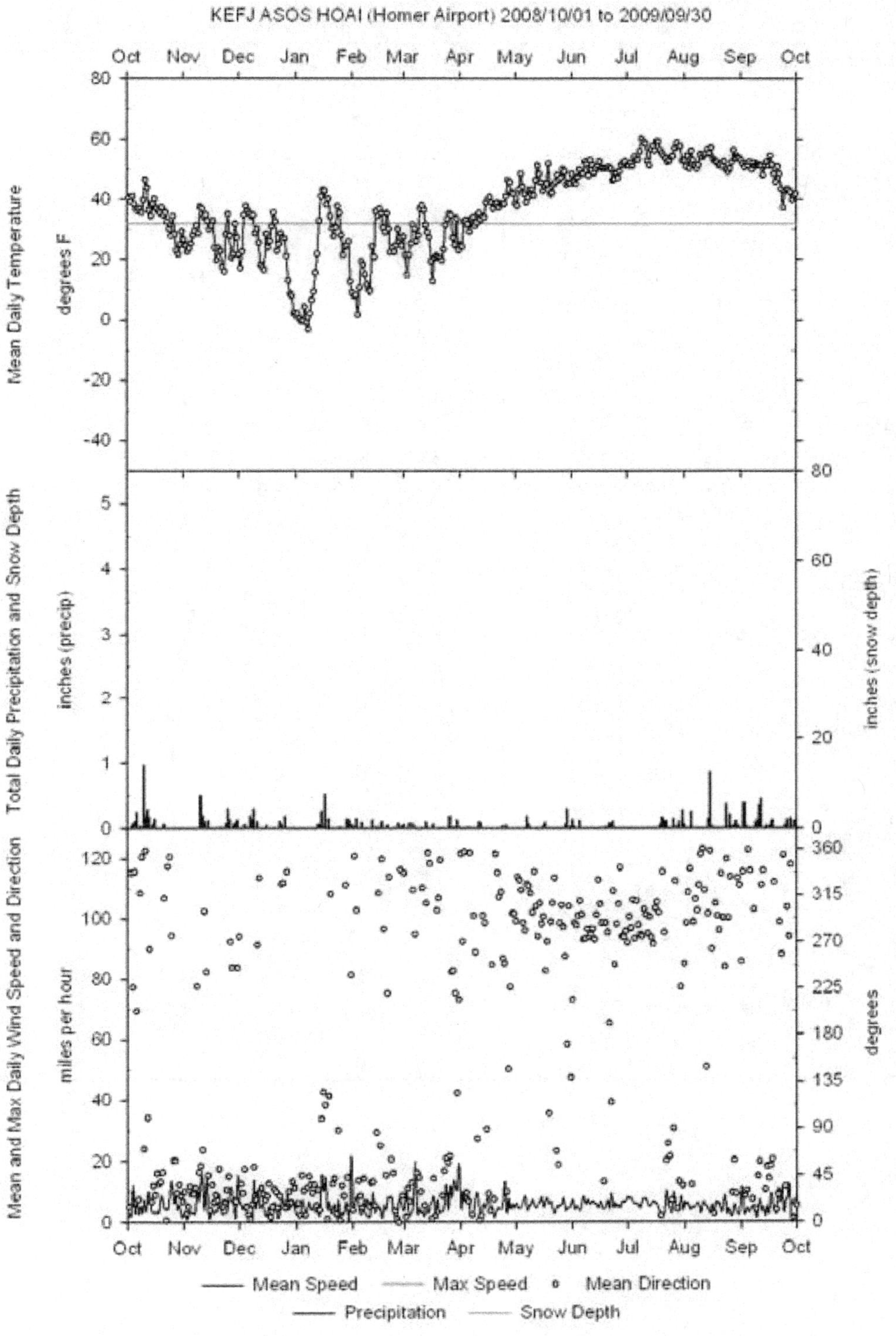
KEFJ ASOS HOAI (Homer Airport) 2008/10/01 to 2009/09/30
Oct Nov Dec Jan Feb Mar Apr May Jun Jul Aug Sep Oct
Mean Daily Temperature
degrees F
80 60 40 20 0 -20 -40
Total Daily Precipitation and Snow Depth
inches (precip)
5 4 3 2 1 0
inches (snow depth)
80 60 40 20 0
Mean and Max Daily Wind Speed and Direction
miles per hour
120 100 80 60 40 20 0
degrees
360 315 270 225 180 135 90 45 0
Mean Speed
Max Speed
Mean Direction
Precipitation
Snow Depth

2009 Hydrologic Year – KEFJ ASOS SEAl (Seward Airport)												
	Oct	Nov	Dec	Jan	Feb	Mar	Apr	May	Jun	Jul	Aug	Sep	Year
Minimum air temperature (°F)												
Min.	16	17	5	-4	1	9.5	17	31	37	43	41	32	-4
Max.	43	33	33	35.3	36	32	40	45	49	60	52	50	60
Mean	30.1	24.1	19.2	16.8	19.7	23	30.2	38.8	44.2	50.2	48	42.8	32.3
# days < 32 °F	16	27	29	25	24	28	17	1	0	0	0	0	167
% valid obs	100	99.9	100	100	100	100	100	100	100	100	100	100	100
Maximum air temperature (°F)												
Min.	29	20	9	2	9	17	36	43	47	51	54	47	2
Max.	50	41	38	49	38	42	53	66	74	84	67	65	84
Mean	41.3	31.9	27.5	25.6	29.6	33.4	42.6	52.6	56.4	61.3	58.6	54	43
# days < 32 °F	2	13	21	18	12	9	0	0	0	0	0	0	75
% valid obs	100	99.9	100	100	100	100	100	100	100	100	100	100	100
Mean air temperature (°F)												
Observed	35.2	27.8	23.5	21	24.5	28.3	36.6	46.3	50.9	55.6	53.3	48.4	37.7
% valid obs	100	99.9	100	100	100	100	100	100	100	100	100	100	100
POR mean												
1971-2000												
Precipitation (in)												
Total*	6.01	4.01	1.36	9.7	1.04	1.19	1.99	1.25	1.67	9.95	3.78	3.58	45.53
% valid obs	100	99.9	100	100	100	100	100	100	100	100	100	100	100
POR mean												
1971-2000												
Snow depth (in)												
Average												
% valid obs												
POR mean												
Wind (mph, degrees)												
Mean speed	9	11.4	12.2	11.6	12.2	11.2	7	6.7	6.2	5.7	4.9	5.9	
% valid obs	99.9	98.1	100	97.8	100	99.9	100	100	100	100	100	100	
Max speed												
Max direction												
Solar radiation (KWh/m²)												
Total												
% valid obs												

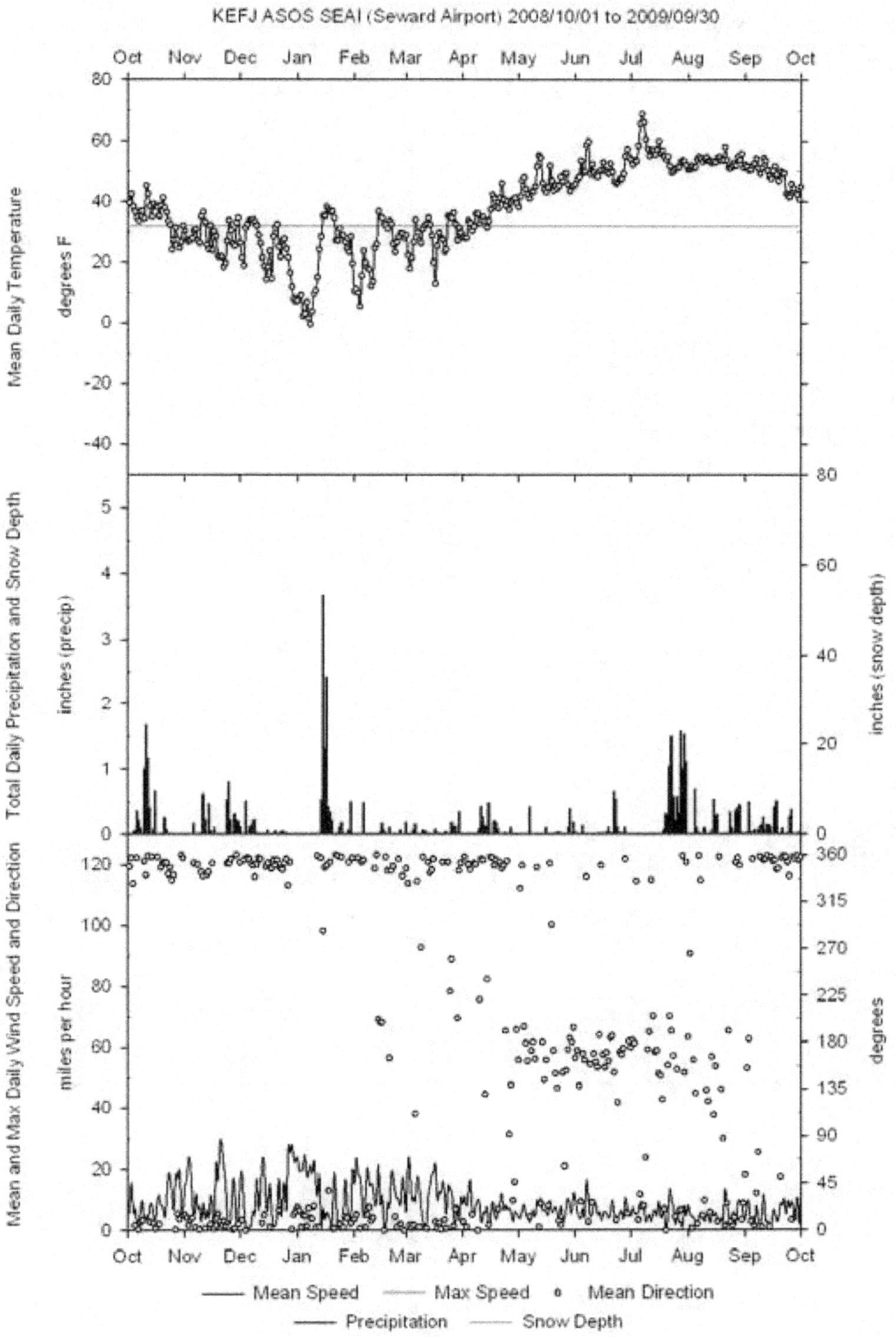

KEFJ ASOS SEAI (Seward Airport) 2008/10/01 to 2009/09/30

2009 Hydrologic Year – KEFJ CMAN PIRO (Pilot Rock)

	Oct	Nov	Dec	Jan	Feb	Mar	Apr	May	Jun	Jul	Aug	Sep	Year
Minimum air temperature (°F)													
Min.	25	27.3	16.7	11.7	10.9	18.5	29.1	34.5	43.3	50.5	49.3	42.6	10.9
Max.	45.7	52.7	45.7	39.4	34	35.4	42.1	49.6	56.3	62.8	54	51.8	62.8
Mean	37.5	36.1	32.1	27.3	28.2	29.2	34.4	43.1	47.6	55.8	51.7	48.7	39.4
# days < 32 °F	4	4	14	17	19	22	9	0	0	0	0	0	89
% valid obs	100	99.9	99.9	99.6	99.7	99	99.7	100	100	100	100	99.4	99.8
Maximum air temperature (°F)													
Min.	33.3	33.4	19.8	16.3	18.1	25.2	34.3	40.8	47.1	53.1	53.8	48.6	16.3
Max.	51.6	65.3	52.7	42.4	40.5	41.9	50.5	56.3	64.6	78.3	64.2	59.7	78.3
Mean	43.9	43	37.5	32.9	33.7	35	40.4	48.6	53.3	61.1	57.3	54.3	45.2
# days < 32 °F	0	0	5	12	7	4	0	0	0	0	0	0	28
% valid obs	100	99.9	99.9	99.6	99.7	99	99.7	100	100	100	100	99.4	99.8
Mean air temperature (°F)													
Observed	40.6	39.1	34.6	29.8	30.4	31.8	36.8	45.4	49.8	57.9	54	51	41.9
% valid obs	100	99.9	99.9	99.6	99.7	99	99.7	100	100	100	100	99.4	99.8
POR mean													
1971-2000													
Precipitation (in)													
Total													
% valid obs													
POR mean													
1971-2000													
Snow depth (in)													
Average													
% valid obs													
POR mean													
Wind (mph, degrees)													
Mean speed	17.1	20.5	21.5	23	19.4	19.4	11	8.3	7.3	10.2	7.3	12.7	
% valid obs	100	99.9	99.9	99.7	99.7	99	99.7	100	100	100	100	99.4	
Max speed	48.8	59.1	62.6	61.5	54.6	66	40.7	43.4	42.3	50.1	33.6	45.4	
Max direction													
Solar radiation (KWh/m^2)													
Total													
% valid obs													

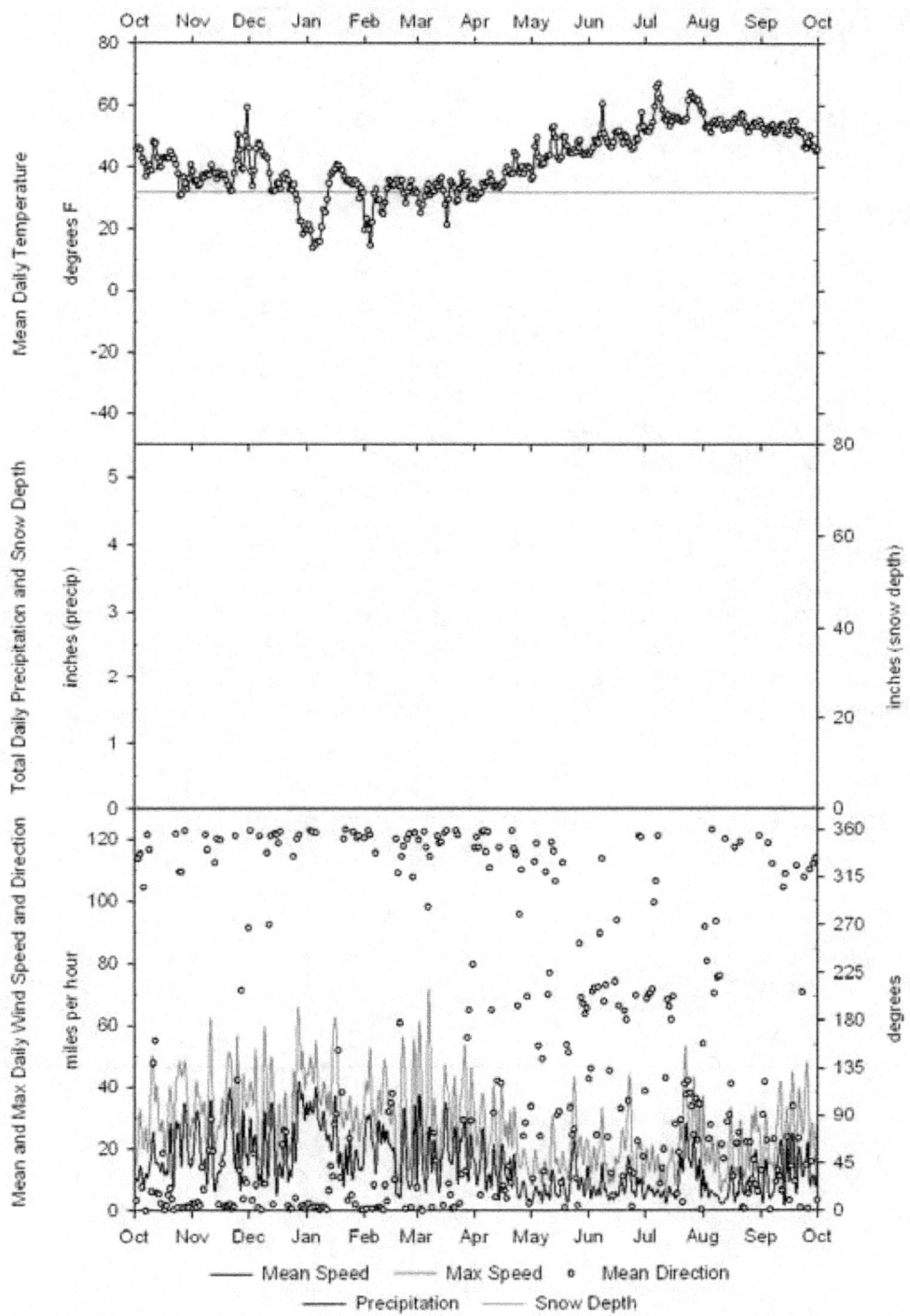

KEFJ CMAN PIRO (Pilot Rock) 2008/10/01 to 2009/09/30

Mean and Max Daily Wind Speed and Direction   Total Daily Precipitation and Snow Depth   Mean Daily Temperature

— Mean Speed   — Max Speed   ○ Mean Direction
— Precipitation   — Snow Depth

2009 Hydrologic Year – KEFJ COOP HOAI (Homer Airport)

	Oct	Nov	Dec	Jan	Feb	Mar	Apr	May	Jun	Jul	Aug	Sep	Year
Minimum air temperature (°F)													
Min.	13	9	-5	-9	-9	2	15	30	36	39	38	26	-9
Max.	39	35	33	40	35	36	43	45	47	53	54	49	54
Mean	27.7	20.8	17.7	13.8	14.6	20.2	29.2	35.3	41	48	45.6	40.6	29.6
# days < 32 °F	23	27	27	25	26	26	23	6	0	0	0	2	185
% valid obs	100	100	100	100	100	100	100	100	100	100	100	100	100
Maximum air temperature (°F)													
Min.	30	22	9	3	9	18	30	44	50	55	53	46	3
Max.	52	42	44	48	40	41	54	67	71	67	66	63	71
Mean	41.1	33	29.7	27.1	29.6	32.6	42.9	53.3	57.7	61.3	59.9	54.5	43.6
# days < 32 °F	1	11	16	17	13	9	1	0	0	0	0	0	68
% valid obs	100	100	100	100	100	100	100	100	100	100	100	100	100
Mean air temperature (°F)													
Observed	34.5	26.9	23.8	20.5	22.1	26.4	36	44.3	49.4	54.6	52.8	47.6	36.7
% valid obs	100	100	100	100	100	100	100	100	100	100	100	100	100
POR mean[1]	37.9	29.0	24.2	22.9	25.5	28.6	36.1	43.2	49.7	53.6	53.3	47.6	37.6
1971-2000	37.8	29.4	25.8	23.4	24.9	29.4	36.4	43.7	50.0	54.1	53.8	47.9	38.1
Precipitation (in)													
Total	2.26	1.71	1.15	1.47	0.69	0.67	0.32	0.83	0.41	0.95	2.05	2.46	14.97
% valid obs	100	100	100	100	100	100	100	100	100	100	100	100	100
POR mean[1]	3.12	2.76	2.82	2.26	1.74	1.53	1.19	0.99	0.96	1.55	2.46	3.05	24.43
1971-2000	2.77	2.87	3.00	2.61	2.04	1.82	1.21	1.07	0.96	1.45	2.28	3.37	25.45
Snow depth (in)													
Average													
% valid obs													
POR mean[1]	0	1	4	4	5	5	2	0	0	0	0	0	
Wind (mph, degrees)													
Mean speed													
% valid obs													
Max speed													
Max direction													
Solar radiation (KWh/m^2)													
Total													
% valid obs													

[1]Period of record used: 9/01/1932 to12/31/2009

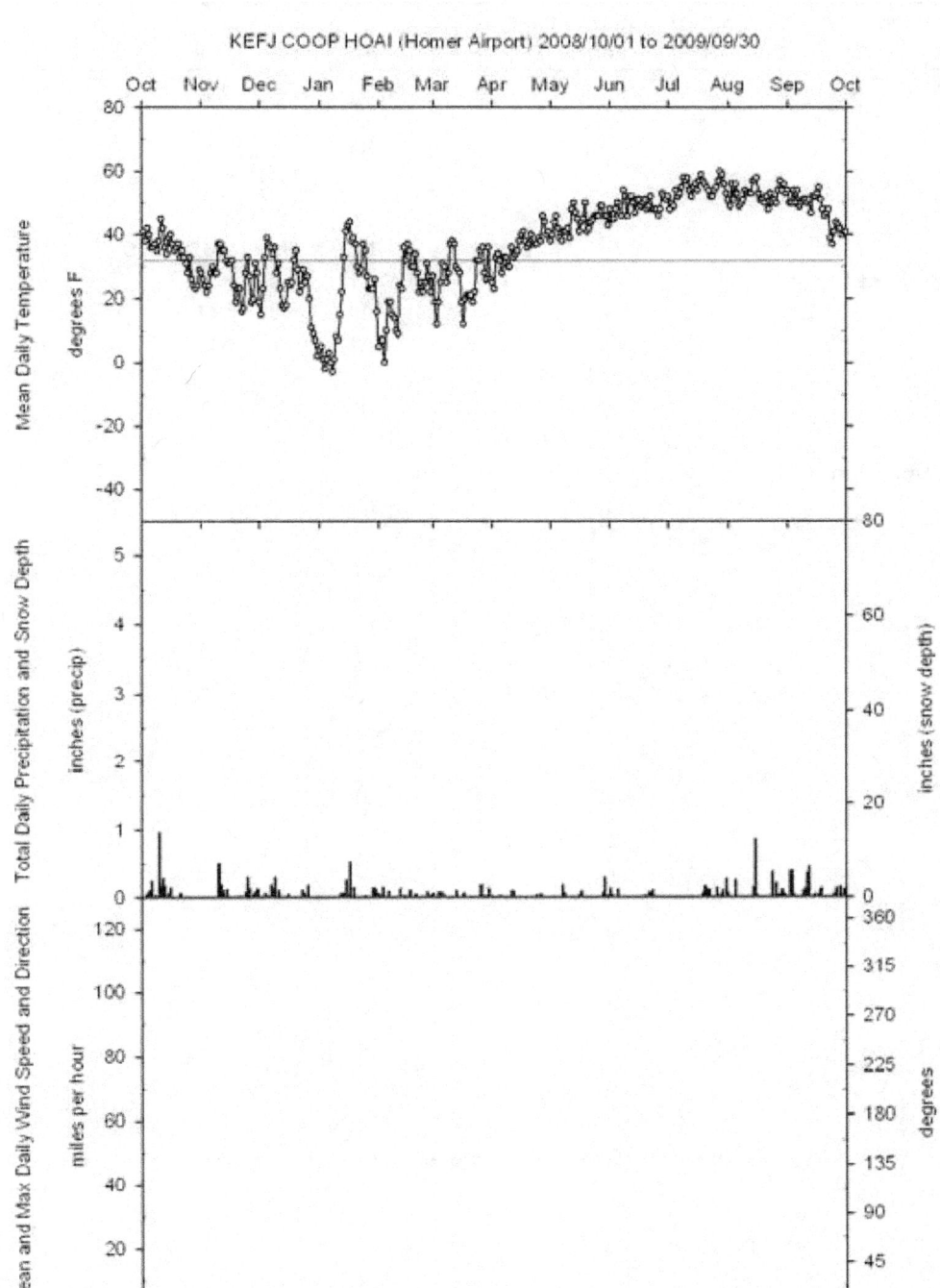

KEFJ COOP HOAI (Homer Airport) 2008/10/01 to 2009/09/30

2009 Hydrologic Year – KEFJ COOP S8NW (Seward 8 NW)													
	Oct	Nov	Dec	Jan	Feb	Mar	Apr	May	Jun	Jul	Aug	Sep	Year
Minimum air temperature (°F)													
Min.	2	-4	-18	-26	-13	-5	2	24	31		24		-26
Max.	33	31	31	31	32	30	33	49	46		48		49
Mean	20.7	12.7	5.4	1.3	7	11.9	21.1	33.2	38.6		39.7		19.8
# days < 32 °F	29	27	30	22	24	24	23	10	4		2		195
% valid obs	96.8	90	96.8	71	92.9	77.4	83.3	77.4	96.7	0	100	0	73.4
Maximum air temperature (°F)													
Min.	27	19	-8	-6	6	23	38	49	48		56		-8
Max.	53	40	38	50	46	42	61	72	78		76		78
Mean	40.7	30.5	22.3	19.9	29.9	36.4	46.6	61.3	65.5		64.5		42.7
# days < 32 °F	5	12	19	14	9	5	0	0	0		0		64
% valid obs	93.5	80	90.3	71	89.3	77.4	80	77.4	100	0	100	0	71.5
Mean air temperature (°F)													
Observed	31	21.7	14.1	10.5	18.9	24.2	33.8	47.3	52.3		52.2		31.5
% valid obs	93.5	80	90.3	71	89.3	77.4	80	77.4	96.7	0	100	0	71.5
POR mean													
1971-2000													
Precipitation (in)													
Total	9.46	5.71	1.54	3.14	1.13	1.76	1.13	0.38	2.04		7.94		34.24
% valid obs	100	86.7	93.5	64.5	82.1	67.7	80	87.1	100	0	100	0	71.8
POR mean													
1971-2000													
Snow depth (in)													
Average	1	17	29	31	40	43	41	0	0		0		
% valid obs	100	93.3	96.8	71	85.7	77.4	83.3	77.4	100	0	100	0	
POR mean													
Wind (mph, degrees)													
Mean speed													
% valid obs													
Max speed													
Max direction													
Solar radiation (KWh/m^2)													
Total													
% valid obs													

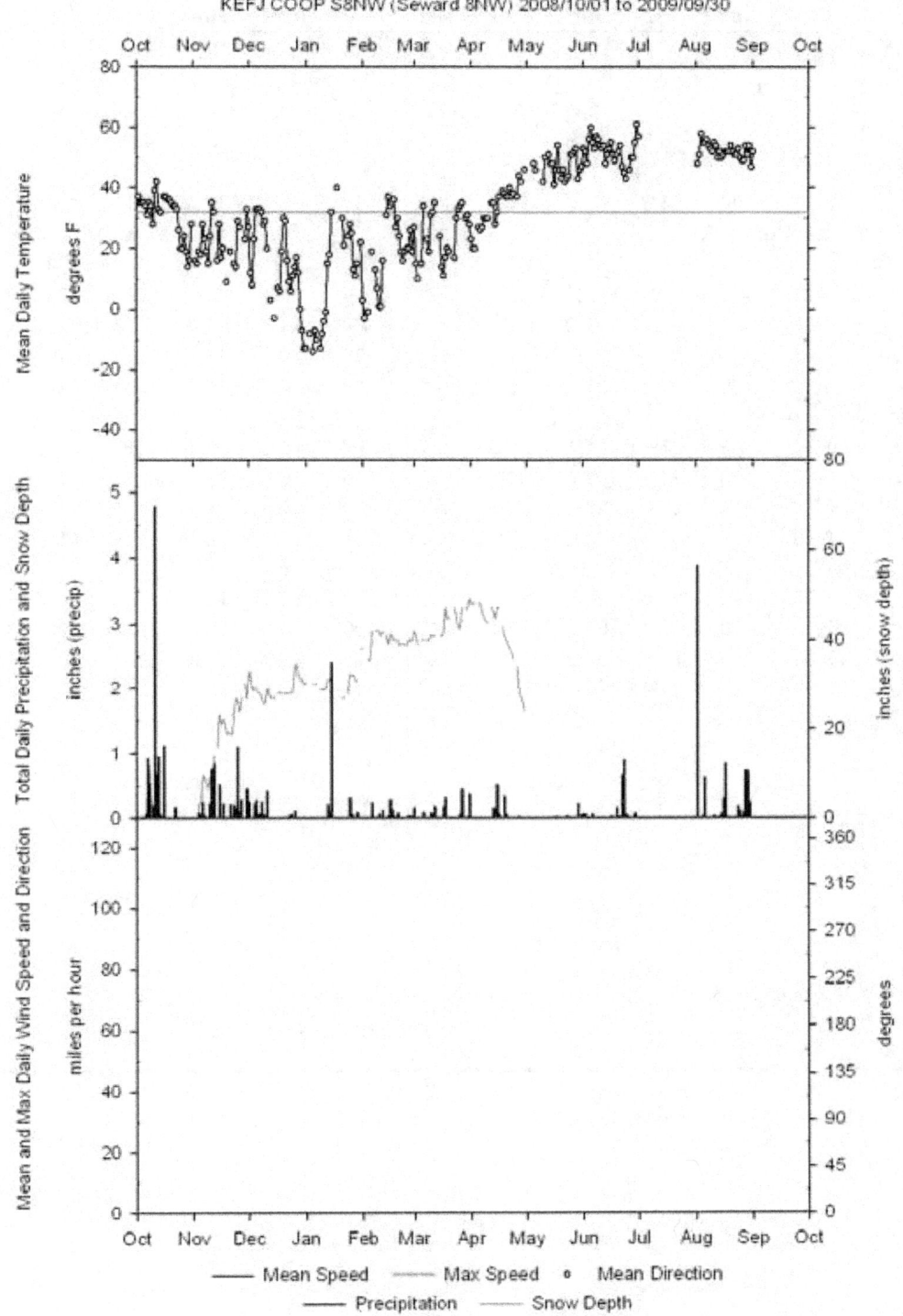

KEFJ COOP S8NW (Seward 8NW) 2008/10/01 to 2009/09/30

59

2009 Hydrologic Year – KEFJ COOP SEWA (Seward)												
	Oct	Nov	Dec	Jan	Feb	Mar	Apr	May	Jun	Jul	Aug	Sep	Year
Minimum air temperature (°F)													
Min.	15	16	4	-4	1	9	17	30	36	42	40	32	-4
Max.	39	33	33	34	35	32	38	45	48	60	52	50	60
Mean	28.9	23.4	18.3	15.9	19	22.6	29.6	38.4	43.8	49.7	47.5	42.4	31.8
# days < 32 °F	18	28	28	24	25	30	19	2	0	0	0	0	174
% valid obs	90.3	100	96.8	96.8	100	100	100	100	96.7	100	100	100	98.4
Maximum air temperature (°F)													
Min.	30	20	9	2	10	18	36	43	48	51	54	48	2
Max.	50	42	38	50	39	42	53	68	76	85	68	65	85
Mean	41.7	32.3	27.7	25.9	30	33.8	43	53.3	57.4	62.3	59.4	54.7	43.6
# days < 32 °F	1	13	20	17	11	7	0	0	0	0	0	0	69
% valid obs	90.3	100	96.8	96.8	100	100	100	100	100	100	100	100	98.6
Mean air temperature (°F)													
Observed	35.2	27.9	23.1	21.1	24.5	28.3	36.4	45.9	50.7	56	53.5	48.5	37.7
% valid obs	90.3	100	96.8	96.8	100	100	100	100	96.7	100	100	100	98.4
POR mean[1]	39.6	31.1	26.6	25.2	27.5	31.1	38.1	45.5	51.9	56.1	55.7	49.5	39.8
1971-2000	39.8	31.7	28.1	26.2	27.2	32.0	38.6	45.8	52.1	56.4	55.9	49.6	40.3
Precipitation (in)													
Total	5.57	3.48	1.16	9.2	1.04	1.19	2	1.26	1.66	9.95	3.72	3.59	43.82
% valid obs	93.5	100	90.3	93.5	96.4	96.8	100	100	96.7	100	83.9	96.7	95.6
POR mean[1]	9.94	7.17	7.57	6.15	5.77	3.81	4.05	3.92	2.30	2.63	5.16	10.13	68.6
1971-2000	9.81	7.15	7.84	7.19	5.82	4.14	4.71	4.75	2.32	2.24	5.49	10.36	71.82
Snow depth (in)													
Average													
% valid obs													
POR mean[1]	0	1	4	6	8	7	2	0	0	0	0	0	
Wind (mph, degrees)													
Mean speed													
% valid obs													
Max speed													
Max direction													
Solar radiation (KWh/m²)													
Total													
% valid obs													

[1]Period of record used: 9/01/1949 to 9/30/2008

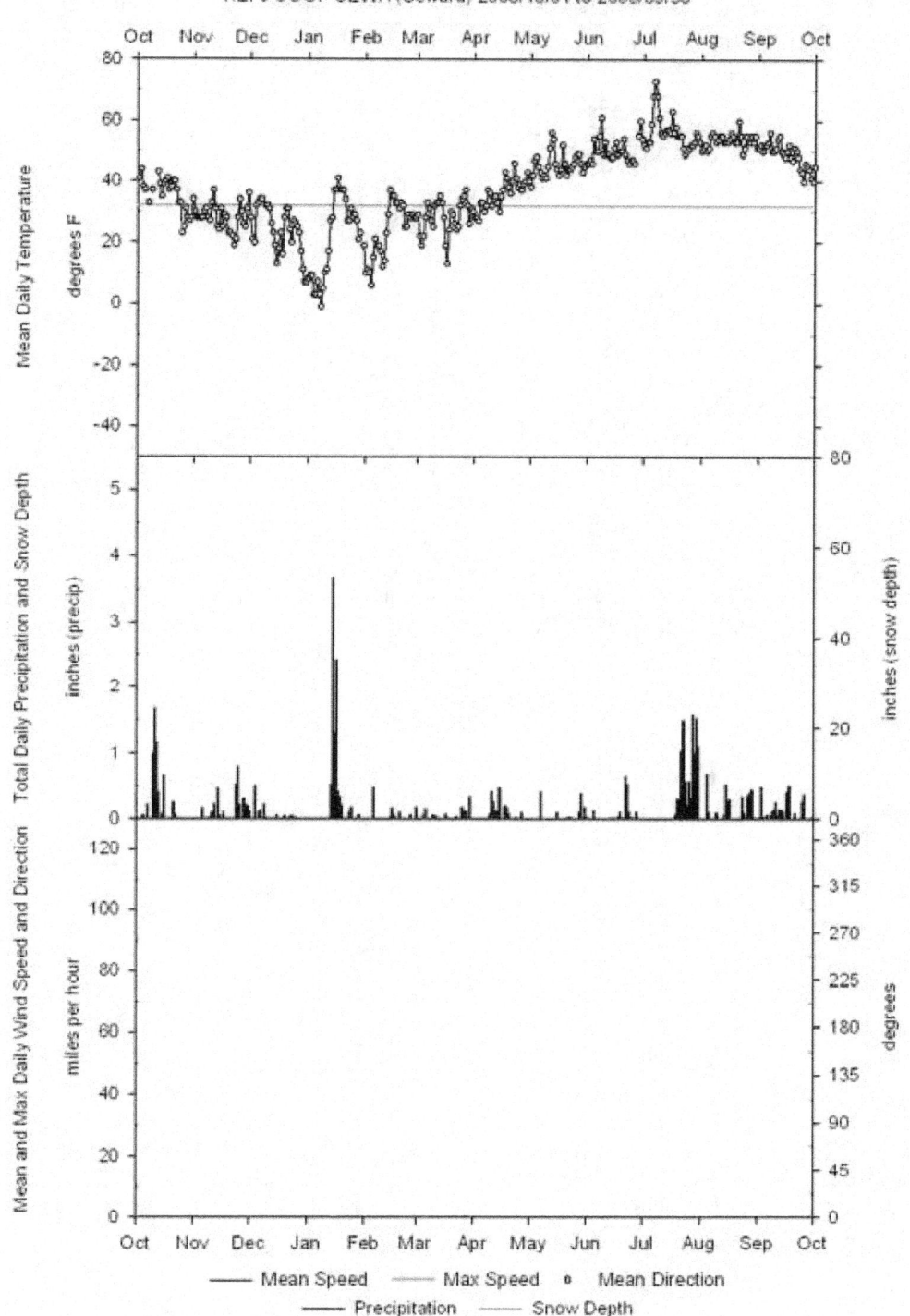

KEFJ COOP SEWA (Seward) 2008/10/01 to 2009/09/30

Mean Speed ── Max Speed ── o Mean Direction
Precipitation ── Snow Depth

61

2009 Hydrologic Year – KEFJ RAWS HAIC (Harding Icefield)

	Oct	Nov	Dec	Jan	Feb	Mar	Apr	May	Jun	Jul	Aug	Sep	Year
Minimum air temperature (°F)													
Min.	0.5	1.9	-7.8	-17.5	-19.3	-7.6	2.8	22.6	26.6	33.4	33.1	18.5	-19.3
Max.	28.4	23.2	27	24.4	26.2	19	32.9	39.4	42.6	58.6	42.8	41.7	58.6
Mean	16.6	12.6	10.2	6.8	6.9	7.8	17.1	29.4	33.4	42.9	37.7	31.2	21.1
# days < 32 °F	31	30	31	31	28	31	29	20	12	0	0	12	255
% valid obs	100	100	100	100	100	100	100	100	94	99.9	100	94.7	99.1
Maximum air temperature (°F)													
Min.	8.4	14.2	1.6	-8.5	-6.5	1.4	12.9	30.6	31.3	35.4	39.2	27.1	-8.5
Max.	38.8	26.6	32.2	31.6	39.4	33.4	55.4	64.8	62.1	73.2	54.9	53.6	73.2
Mean	25.4	20.3	18.1	15.6	18.2	19.8	30.0	45.3	44.8	52.1	46.3	38.1	31.2
# days < 32 °F	30	30	30	30	25	29	19	4	1	0	0	5	203
% valid obs	100	100	100	100	100	100	100	100	94	99.9	100	94.7	99.1
Mean air temperature (°F)													
Observed	20.4	16.8	13.7	11.2	12.2	13.2	22.2	35.1	38.2	46.6	41.4	34.3	25.4
% valid obs	100	100	100	100	100	100	100	100	94.2	99.9	100	94.7	99.1
POR mean													
1971-2000													
Precipitation (in)													
Total[2]	0.85	0	0	0	0.21	0.14	1.52	0.48	0.67	7.79	3.27	3.88	18.81
% valid obs	98.4	98.8	100	99.9	100	100	100	100	93.9	97.4	100	94.7	98.6
POR mean													
1971-2000													
Snow depth (in)													
Average									6.1				
% valid obs	0	0	0	0	0	0	0	0	25.6	0.1	0	0	
POR average													
Wind (mph, degrees)													
Mean speed	10.9	8.3	5.9	11.5					10.3	15.1	10.7	14.8	
% valid obs	100	100	100	49.2	0	0	0	0	85.6	99.9	100	94.7	
Max speed	124.6	81.2	62	77.2					59.1	83.4	64.4	65.8	124.6
Max direction	113	115	115	124					117	98	108	90	113
Solar radiation (KWh/m^2)													
Total	41.1	11.3	4.8	6.9	25.2	66.7	146.9	195.9	227.9	212.9	96.9	69.9	1106.4
% valid obs	100	100	100	100	100	100	100	100	94.2	99.9	100	94.7	99.1

[2] A displacement precipitation gauge (filled with an antifreeze solution) is used at the Harding Icefield RAWS. By design, this gauge is capable of accurately measuring winter-time precipitation. In reality, undercatch (the difference between the actual amount of snow and the amount measured by a precipitation gauge) is a significant problem because of the extremely windy nature of the site. Measured precipitation is only a fraction of the snow water equivalent reflected by the adjacent snowpack.

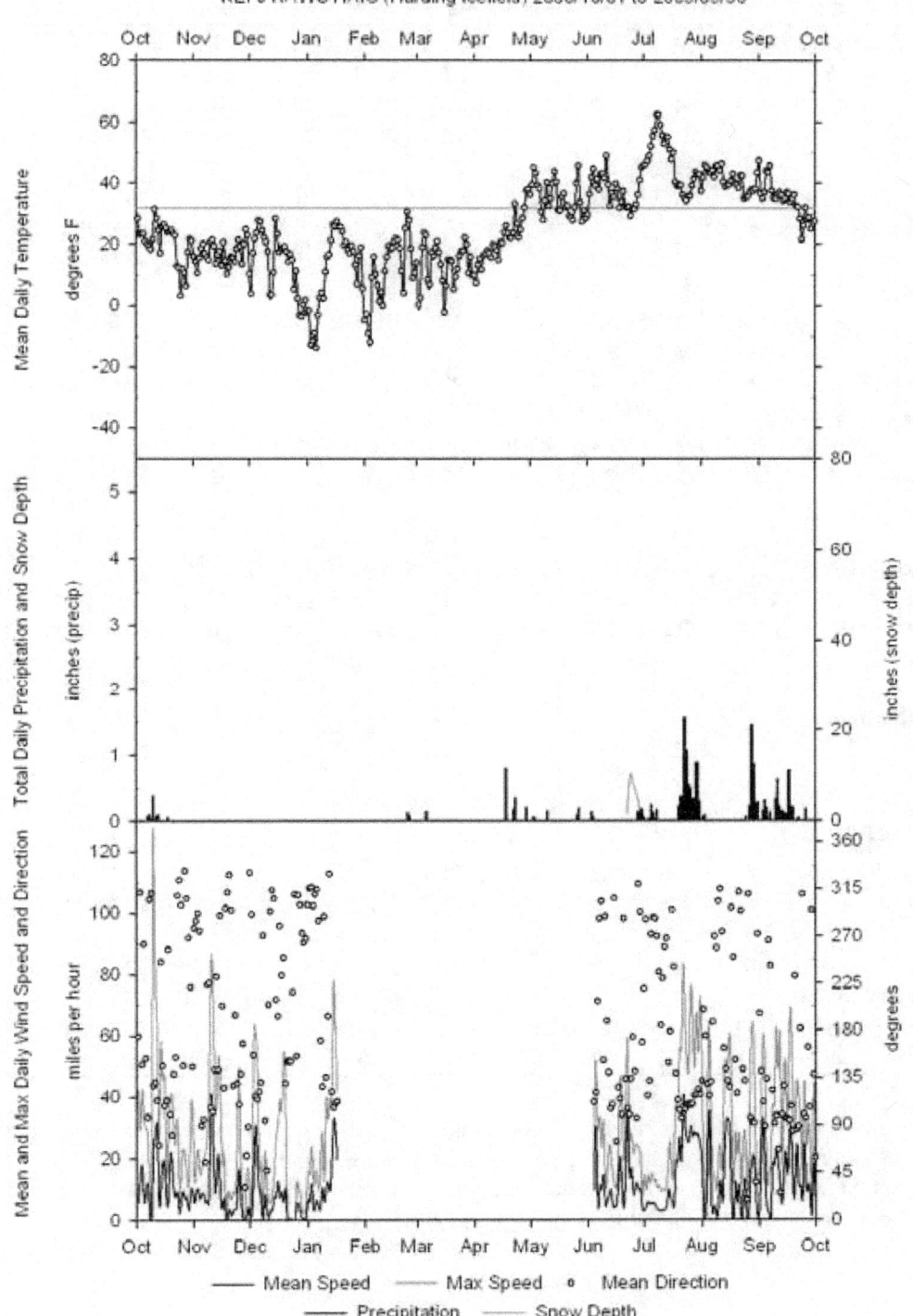

KEFJ RAWS HAIC (Harding Icefield) 2008/10/01 to 2009/09/30

2009 Hydrologic Year – KEFJ RAWS MCPA (McArthur Pass)													
	Oct	Nov	Dec	Jan	Feb	Mar	Apr	May	Jun	Jul	Aug	Sep	Year
Minimum air temperature (°F)													
Min.	18.1	19.8	13.5	3.7	1.8	13.3	21.9	31.5	32	43.5	42.6	34.3	1.8
Max.	40.3	31.8	34	34.3	30.4	29.1	38.3	50	51.4	67.3	52	48.6	67.3
Mean	31.6	27.4	25.2	22.5	22.1	22.5	29.5	37.7	41.2	49.3	46.9	42.4	33.3
# days < 32 °F	16	30	28	28	28	31	22	1	0	0	0	0	184
% valid obs	99.9	100	100	100	100	100	100	100	99.9	99.9	100	100	100
Maximum air temperature (°F)													
Min.	23.9	25.2	21.4	12.7	11.8	21.7	25.9	38.5	40.1	46.8	48	39.6	11.8
Max.	46.4	37	36.3	38.8	41.2	34.9	46.8	60.4	67.5	77.5	63.9	62.4	77.5
Mean	38.3	32.6	29.7	28.2	28.8	29.2	36.4	47.3	52.4	56.6	55.1	49.5	40.4
# days < 32 °F	3	13	23	21	21	25	10	0	0	0	0	0	116
% valid obs	99.9	100	100	100	100	100	100	100	99.9	99.9	100	100	100
Mean air temperature (°F)													
Observed	34.4	30	27.3	25.4	25.2	25.7	32.3	42.1	45.9	52.7	50.2	45.7	36.5
% valid obs	99.9	100	100	100	100	100	100	100	99.9	99.9	100	100	100
POR mean 1971-2000													
Precipitation (in)													
Total[2]	8.93	3.33	1.89	6.16	0.11	0.06	1.25	4.89	5.39	26.16	11.26	13.12	82.55
% valid obs	80.9	45.6	26.2	26.3	9.4	7.1	59.3	100	99.7	95.7	100	96.8	62.5
POR mean 1971-2000													
Snow depth (in)													
Average			1.6	0.1									
% valid obs			2.2	9.1									
POR mean													
Wind (mph, degrees)													
Mean speed	13.5	15	17.1	20.8	13.3	17.5			10.1	15.5	9.5	15.9	
% valid obs	99.9	100	100	100	100	79.6	0	0	94.3	99.9	100	100	
Max speed	71.8	83	92.6	122.8	79.4	107.4			68.2	105.6	64.7	87.7	122.8
Max direction		103	114	111	105	306			115	133	112	116	111
Solar radiation (KWh/m^2)													
Total	41.5	14.9	7.1	12	33.1	66.8	110.2	138.6	151.1	104.7	106.9	59.4	846.3
% valid obs	99.9	100	100	100	100	100	100	100	99.9	99.9	100	100	100

[2]Station is only capable of measuring liquid precipitation. Precipitation reported when maximum air temperature is below 31.1 °F is not considered valid and these data are not used for summarizing purposes. The water equivalent of solid precipitation (e.g. snowfall) is not measured and this is reflected in the percentage of valid observations that are reported as a measure of the reliability of cumulative values.

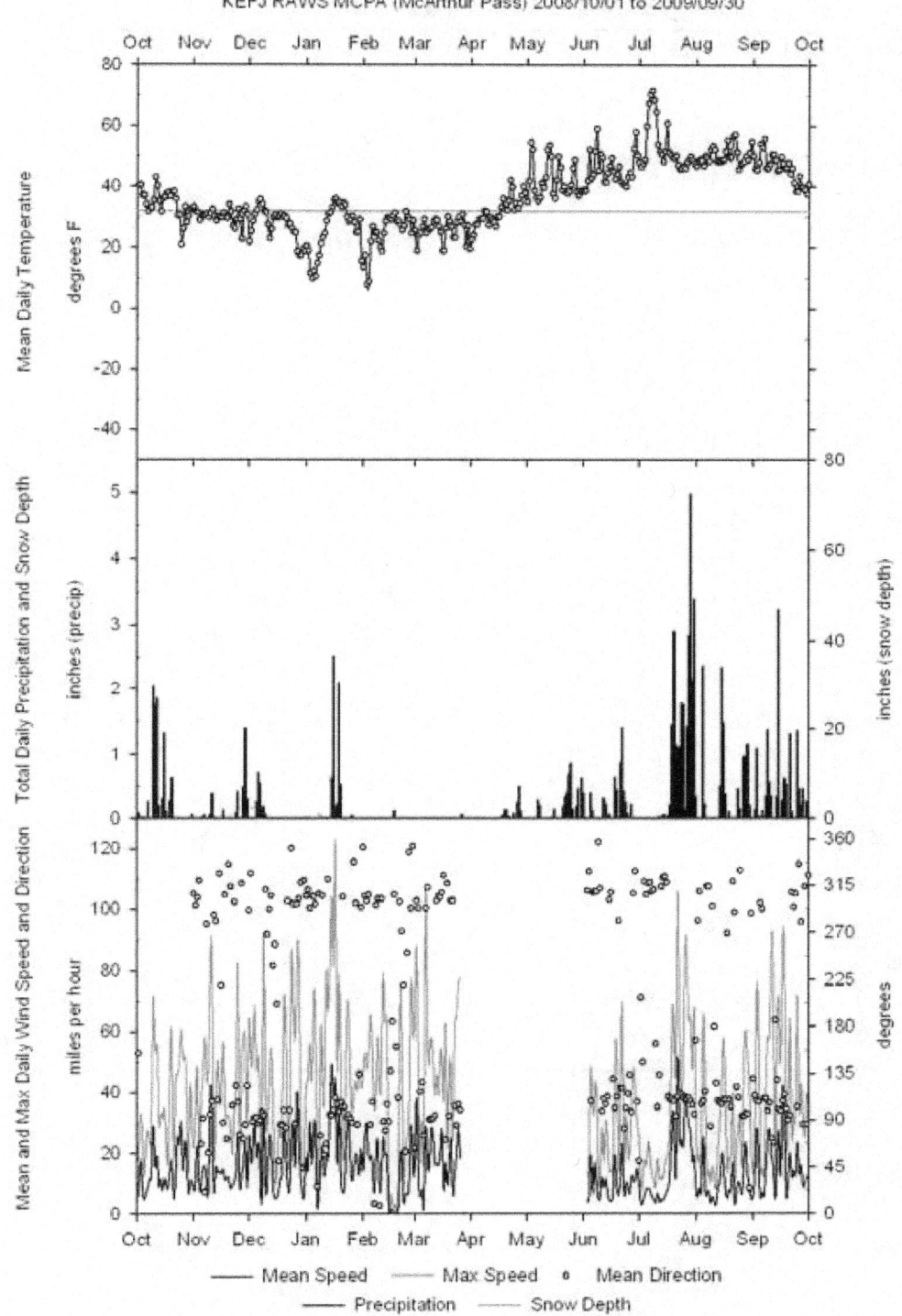

KEFJ RAWS MCPA (McArthur Pass) 2008/10/01 to 2009/09/30

2009 Hydrologic Year – KEFJ SNCO EXGL (Exit Glacier)												
	Oct	Nov	Dec	Jan	Feb	Mar	Apr	May	Jun	Jul	Aug	Sep	Year
Minimum air temperature (°F)												
Min.												
Max.												
Mean												
# days < 32 °F												
% valid obs												
Maximum air temperature (°F)												
Min.												
Max.												
Mean												
# days < 32 °F												
% valid obs												
Mean air temperature (°F)												
Observed												
% valid obs												
POR mean												
1971-2000												
Precipitation (in)												
Total[3]				5.5	8.1	9.4	12.5	8.8				
% valid obs				100	100	100	100	100				
POR mean												
1971-2000												
Snow depth (in)												
Average[4]				26	35	34	47	24				
% valid obs				100	100	100	100	100				
POR mean												
Wind (mph, degrees)												
Mean speed												
% valid obs												
Max speed												
Max direction												
Solar radiation (KWh/m²)												
Total												
% valid obs												

[3]Snow water equivalent measured close to the beginning of the month.
[4]Cumulative snow depth measured close to the beginning of the month.

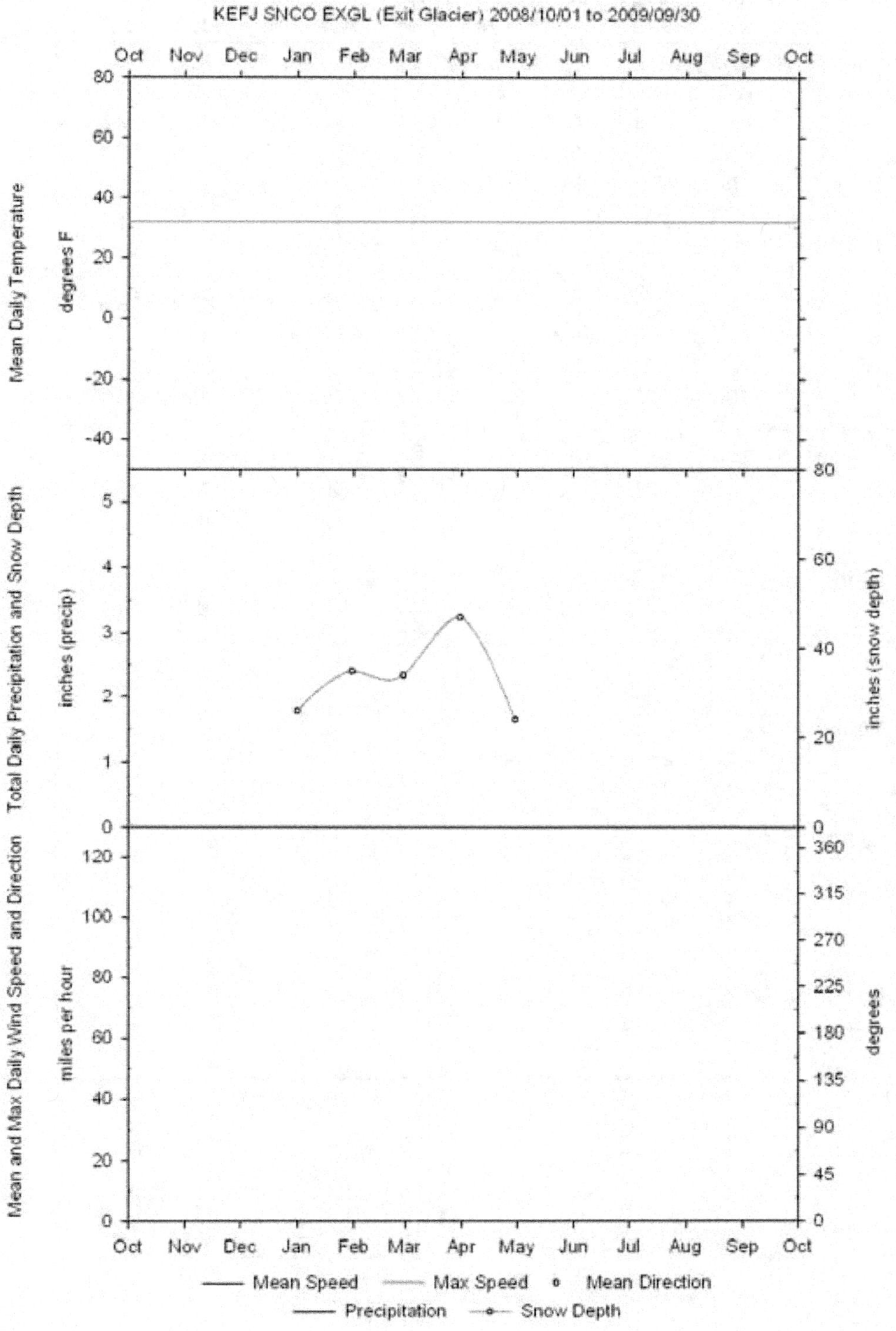

KEFJ SNCO EXGL (Exit Glacier) 2008/10/01 to 2009/09/30

2009 Hydrologic Year – KEFJ SNTE NUGL (Nuka Glacier)													
	Oct	Nov	Dec	Jan	Feb	Mar	Apr	May	Jun	Jul	Aug	Sep	Year
Minimum air temperature (°F)													
Min.	13.3	4.6	-7.8	-13.7	-5.1	-2.6	2.3	27	30.6	37.6	34.3	29.1	-13.7
Max.	39.6	32	33.8	34.9	30	29.1	33.3	39.6	49.3	49.5	47.7	45	49.5
Mean	25.7	17.8	17.1	12.6	13.1	15	23.8	33.9	39.6	45.1	42.3	39.2	27.2
# days < 32 °F	28	29	29	29	28	31	29	8	1	0	0	2	214
% valid obs	100	100	100	100	100	100	100	100	100	100	100	100	100
Maximum air temperature (°F)													
Min.	23.4	16	4.3	-0.2	10.6	9.3	24.3	39	43.7	47.7	48.6	40.6	-0.2
Max.	49.1	40.5	36.7	43.3	33.6	33.6	53.2	65.5	67.3	78.3	67.3	63.7	78.3
Mean	37.4	28.9	26.9	24.9	26.4	27.1	36.7	47.7	54.2	60.2	57.4	50.8	40
# days < 32 °F	5	17	23	20	22	26	6	0	0	0	0	0	119
% valid obs	100	100	100	100	100	100	100	100	100	100	100	100	100
Mean air temperature (°F)													
Observed	31.6	24.4	22.9	19.4	20.5	22	30.7	40.8	47.1	52.9	49.9	44.7	34
% valid obs	100	100	100	100	100	100	100	100	100	100	100	100	100
POR mean													
1971-2000													
Precipitation (in)													
Total	10.4	5.7	2.4	4.1	0.9	1.4	1.8	1.9	4.7	14.8	3.7	9.5	61.3
% valid obs	100	100	100	100	100	100	100	100	100	100	100	100	100
POR mean													
1971-2000													
Snow depth (in)													
Average	0.5	13.8	25.9	31.4	41.6	52	70.2	24.5	0	0	0	0.2	
% valid obs	100	100	100	100	100	100	100	100	100	100	100		
POR mean													
Wind (mph, degrees)													
Mean speed													
% valid obs													
Max speed													
Max direction													
Solar radiation (KWh/m^2)													
Total													
% valid obs													

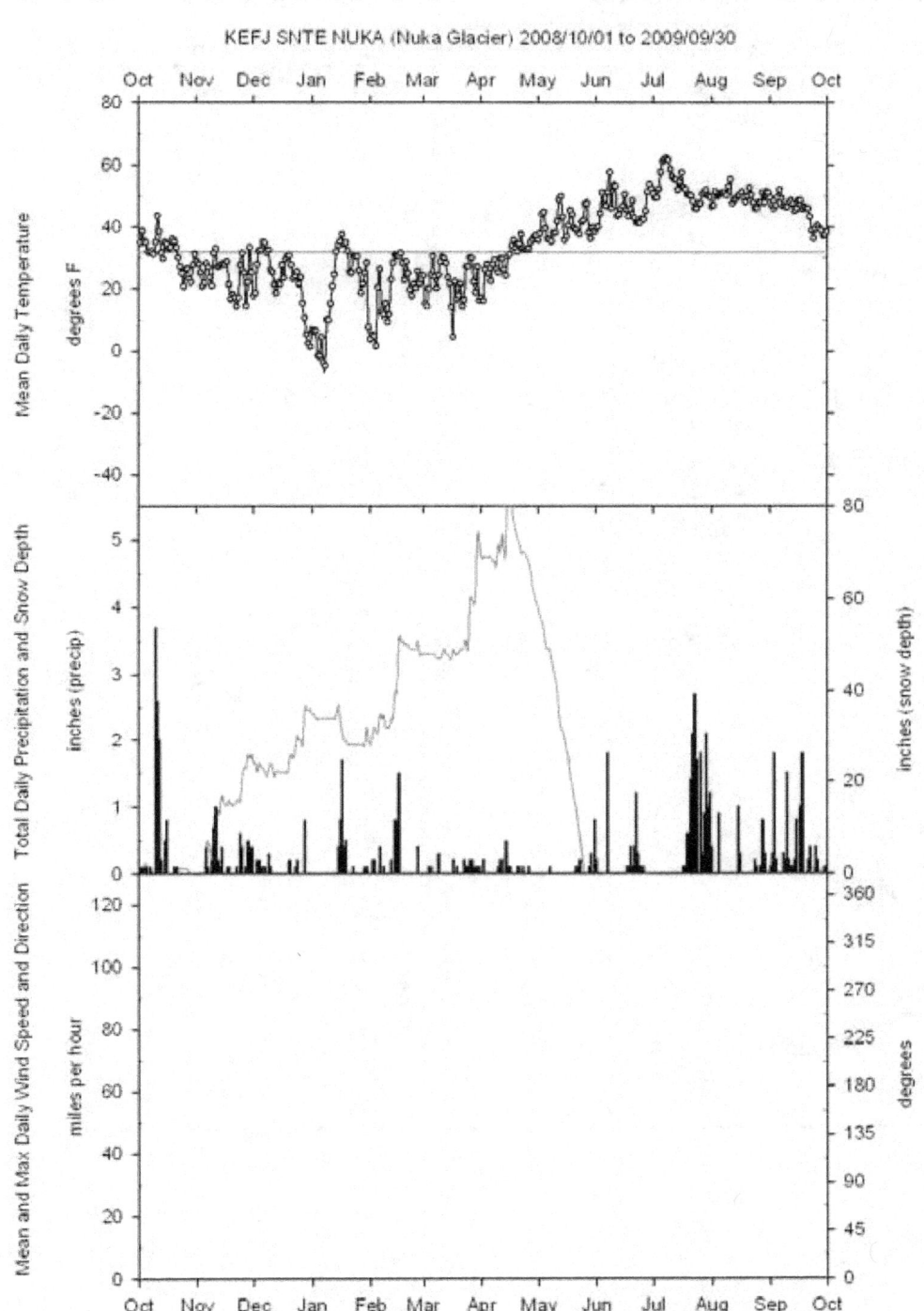

KEFJ SNTE NUKA (Nuka Glacier) 2008/10/01 to 2009/09/30

— Mean Speed   — Max Speed   ∘ Mean Direction
— Precipitation   — Snow Depth

2009 Hydrologic Year – LACL ASOS ILAI (Iliamna Airport)												
	Oct	Nov	Dec	Jan	Feb	Mar	Apr	May	Jun	Jul	Aug	Sep	Year
Minimum air temperature (°F)													
Min.	8	-15	-20	-29	-22	-14	3	28	37	43	40	27	-29
Max.	36	36	38	39	33	33	37.5	42	47	53	54	50	54
Mean	23.1	12.8	14.5	5.8	7.9	8.9	23.9	35.2	42.5	49.6	47.5	41.6	26.3
# days < 32 °F	26	28	24	24	26	30	21	4	0	0	0	4	187
% valid obs	100	100	89.5	100	100	100	100	100	100	100	100	100	99.1
Maximum air temperature (°F)													
Min.	19	-3	-14	-21	-6	-2	20	43	46	53	50	39.3	-21
Max.	49	39	41	47	36	37	46	68	76	77	74	68	77
Mean	35	23.8	25.5	18.7	23.4	21.9	36.4	55.1	57.5	62.6	60.8	53.3	39.6
# days < 32 °F	10	19	16	19	20	23	5	0	0	0	0	0	112
% valid obs	100	100	89.5	100	100	100	100	100	100	100	100	100	99.1
Mean air temperature (°F)													
Observed	29.2	18.4	21.9	12.3	15.8	15.9	30.9	45.3	50.3	56.1	54.1	47.3	33.3
% valid obs	100	100	89.5	100	100	100	100	100	100	100	100	100	99.1
POR mean 1971-2000													
Precipitation (in)													
Total	3.41	1.18	0.85	1.31	1.09	1.43	0.95	1.22	1.2	3.25	1.97	2.9	20.76
% valid obs	100	100	89.5	100	100	100	100	100	100	100	100	100	99.1
POR mean 1971-2000													
Snow depth (in)													
Average													
% valid obs													
POR mean													
Wind (mph, degrees)													
Mean speed	9.6	9.5	10.8	10.9	9.7	10.3	9.3	7.4	8.4	9.4	7.8	7.1	
% valid obs	99.3	100	89.5	100	100	100	100	100	97.8	99.9	100	100	
Max speed													
Max direction													
Solar radiation (KWh/m²)													
Total													
% valid obs													

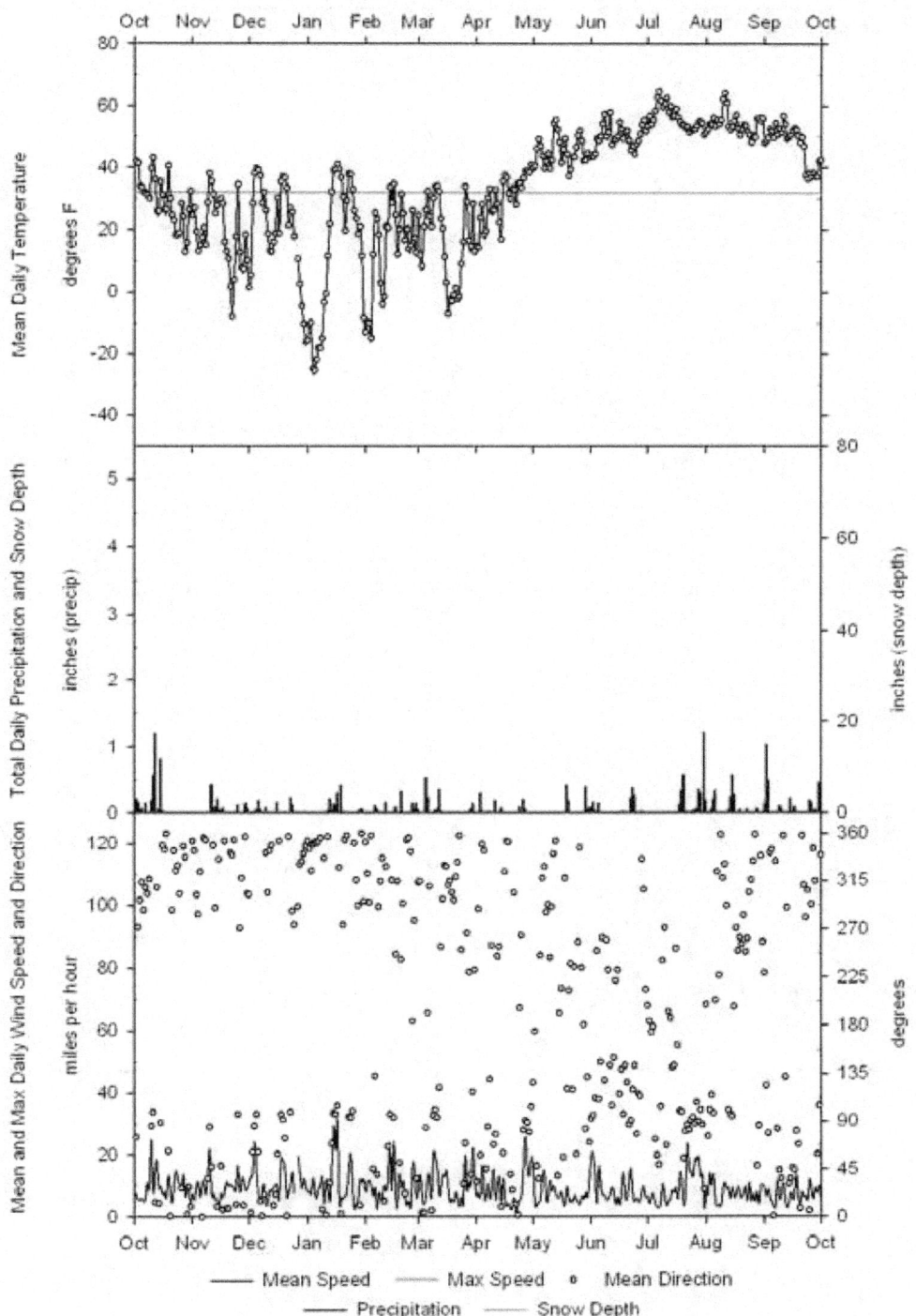

LACL ASOS ILAI (Iliamna Airport) 2008/10/01 to 2009/09/30

Mean Speed — Max Speed — Mean Direction o
Precipitation — Snow Depth —

2009 Hydrologic Year – LACL ASOS KEAI (Kenai Airport)													
	Oct	Nov	Dec	Jan	Feb	Mar	Apr	May	Jun	Jul	Aug	Sep	Year
Minimum air temperature (°F)													
Min.	6	-3	-29	-34	-21	-15	3	30	36	40.4	36.2	26	-34
Max.	42	32	33	36	33	33	39	45	49	56	54	52	56
Mean	25.1	16.4	7	3.5	5.7	13	27.2	37.2	44.2	50.2	47.4	41.3	26.6
# days < 32 °F	24	29	28	27	26	29	16	2	0	0	0	2	183
% valid obs	100	100	100	100	99.9	99.9	100	100	100	100	99.9	100	100
Maximum air temperature (°F)													
Min.	27	17	-9	-12	2	20	30	43.5	51	57	55	45	-12
Max.	54	42	38	45	39	42	63	71	80	73	73	69	80
Mean	38.7	29.7	20.3	18	25.3	30.3	43.6	57.1	60.3	64.4	63.5	57.9	42.5
# days < 32 °F	5	18	24	23	18	19	1	0	0	0	0	0	108
% valid obs	100	100	100	100	99.9	99.9	100	100	100	100	99.9	100	100
Mean air temperature (°F)													
Observed	31.9	23.8	14.1	10.4	16.6	22.5	35.9	48	52.6	57.5	55.9	50.5	35.1
% valid obs	100	100	100	100	99.9	99.9	100	100	100	100	99.9	100	100
POR mean													
1971-2000													
Precipitation (in)													
Total	2.63	0.34	0.36	1.36	0.54	0.38	0.11	0.68	0.95	1.13	2.3	1.47	12.25
% valid obs	100	100	100	100	99.9	99.9	100	100	100	100	100	100	100
POR mean													
1971-2000													
Snow depth (in)													
Average													
% valid obs													
POR mean													
Wind (mph, degrees)													
Mean speed	6.6	7.6	7.8	6.5	5.3	9.2	7.5	7.9	7.9	7.9	6.4	6.8	
% valid obs	100	100	100	99.7	99.9	99.7	100	99.9	100	100	100	100	
Max speed													
Max direction													
Solar radiation (KWh/m^2)													
Total													
% valid obs													

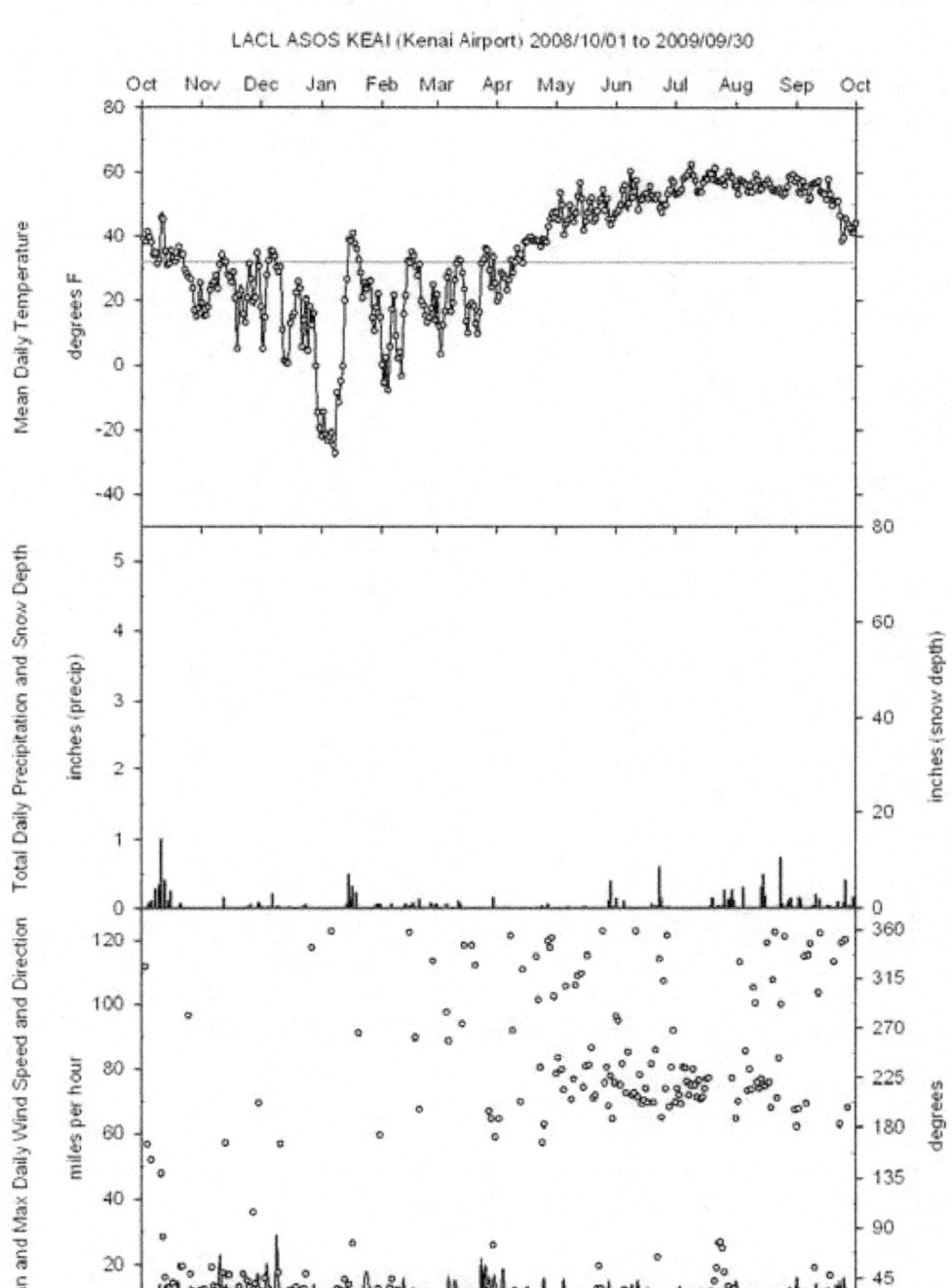

2009 Hydrologic Year – LACL CMAN DRRI (Drift River Terminal)

	Oct	Nov	Dec	Jan	Feb	Mar	Apr	May	Jun	Jul	Aug	Sep	Year
Minimum air temperature (°F)													
Min.	20.5	12.2	-0.2	-8.1	-3.5	3.4	18.7	32.5	41	44.2	44.8	35.4	-8.1
Max.	38.5	34.5	34.5	34.9	31.1	31.5	39.9	46.6	51.3	54.9	54	52.2	54.9
Mean	29.7	23.2	19	13.8	15.5	19.4	31	39.9	44.8	50	49.7	45.6	31.9
# days < 32 °F	19	27	28	27	28	31	15	0	0	0	0	0	175
% valid obs	99.8	99.9	99.8	98.9	99.9	100	100	99.9	100	100	99.9	99.9	99.8
Maximum air temperature (°F)													
Min.	28.8	19.4	6.4	3.6	3.2	19.4	27.3	40.6	46.6	50.2	51.6	43.7	3.2
Max.	47.8	39.7	39.6	40.8	35.2	39.7	52.9	62.1	65.7	62.6	64.9	63.7	65.7
Mean	38.2	31.3	26.1	22	24.7	28.7	39.1	51.4	53.8	56.4	57	53.5	40.3
# days < 32 °F	7	17	22	22	20	23	4	0	0	0	0	0	115
% valid obs	99.8	99.9	99.8	98.9	99.9	100	100	99.9	100	100	99.9	99.9	99.8
Mean air temperature (°F)													
Observed	33.4	26.9	22.4	18.2	19.9	23.8	34.6	44.7	48.3	52.7	53.1	49.1	35.7
% valid obs	99.8	99.9	99.8	98.9	99.9	100	100	99.9	100	100	99.9	99.9	99.8
POR mean													
1971-2000													
Precipitation (in)													
Total													
% valid obs													
POR mean													
1971-2000													
Snow depth (in)													
Average													
% valid obs													
POR mean													
Wind (mph, degrees)													
Mean speed	10	9.8	9.3	8.6	8	9.8	8.3	9.9	8.7	10.5	7.5	9.4	
% valid obs	99.8	99.9	99.8	99.6	99.9	100	100	100	100	100	100	99.9	
Max speed	40.5	41.8	44.1	54.1	30.6	43	30.6	38.7	29.3	35.1	32.9	35.6	
Max direction													
Solar radiation (KWh/m²)													
Total													
% valid obs													

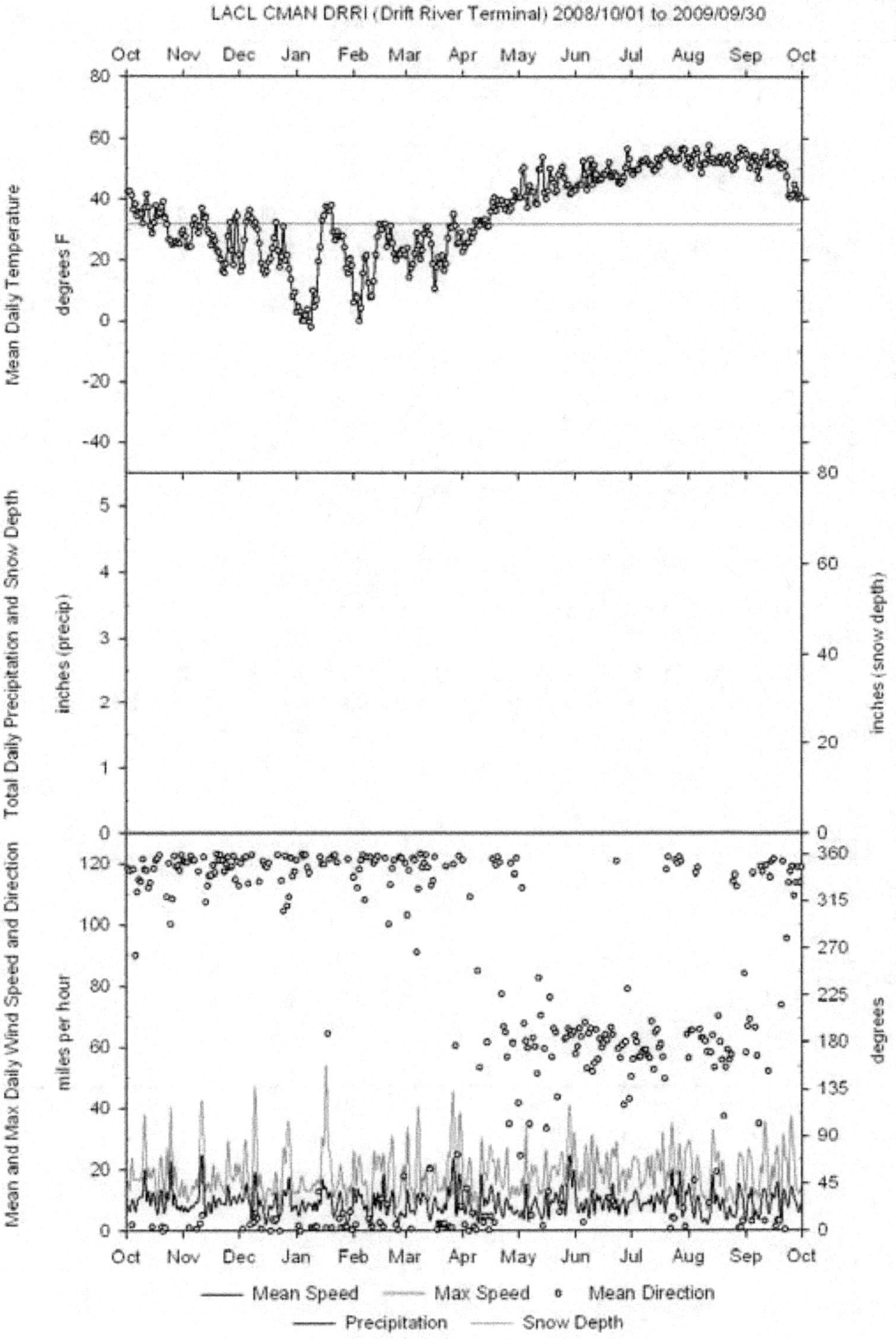

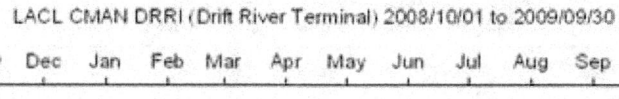

LACL CMAN DRRI (Drift River Terminal) 2008/10/01 to 2009/09/30

2009 Hydrologic Year – LACL COOP ILAI (Iliamna Airport)	Oct	Nov	Dec	Jan	Feb	Mar	Apr	May	Jun	Jul	Aug	Sep	Year
Minimum air temperature (°F)													
Min.	8	-15	-20	-31	-22	-16	2	28	35	42	39	27	-31
Max.	35	36	38	38	33	33	38	42	47	53	52	50	53
Mean	35	36	38	38	33	33	38	42	47	53	52	50	53
# days < 32 °F	26	28	24	24	26	30	21	5	0	0	0	5	189
% valid obs	100	100	83.9	100	100	100	100	100	100	100	100	100	98.6
Maximum air temperature (°F)													
Min.	19	-3	-12	-20	-5	-2	20	44	47	54	52	40	-20
Max.	49	40	42	48	36	37	47	69	76	78	74	69	78
Mean	35.6	24.4	29.1	19.8	24	22.6	36.9	55.9	58.4	63.2	61.7	53.8	40.7
# days < 32 °F	10	18	16	18	20	22	5	0	0	0	0	0	109
% valid obs	100	100	83.9	100	100	100	100	100	100	100	100	100	98.6
Mean air temperature (°F)													
Observed	29.2	18.2	22.8	12.4	15.4	15.3	30.1	45.5	50.1	56.2	54.3	47.5	33.3
% valid obs	100	100	83.9	100	100	100	100	100	100	100	100	100	98.6
POR mean[1]	35.0	24.3	16.9	16.5	18.6	22.2	32.0	43.0	51.2	55.6	54.6	47.9	34.8
1971-2000	34.6	24.9	19.1	16.4	16.4	22.8	32.3	43.1	50.9	55.8	54.5	47.6	34.9
Precipitation (in)													
Total	3.42	1.19	0.85	1.31	1.09	1.44	0.96	1.23	1.2	3.25	1.98	2.91	20.83
% valid obs	100	100	83.9	100	100	100	100	100	100	100	100	100	98.6
POR mean[1]	3.09	2.00	1.56	1.32	1.15	1.12	1.05	1.18	1.50	2.62	4.55	4.40	25.54
1971-2000	3.10	2.25	1.66	1.33	0.98	1.03	0.97	1.27	1.54	2.38	4.26	4.32	25.09
Snow depth (in)													
Average	0	7	7	6	13	11	12	0	0	0	0	0	
% valid obs	100	100	83.9	100	100	100	100	100	100	100	100	100	
POR mean[1]	0	2	4	8	9	10	7	1	0	0	0	0	
Wind (mph, degrees)													
Mean speed													
% valid obs													
Max speed													
Max direction													
Solar radiation (KWh/m^2)													
Total													
% valid obs													

[1]Period of record used: 11/10/1939 to 12/31/2009

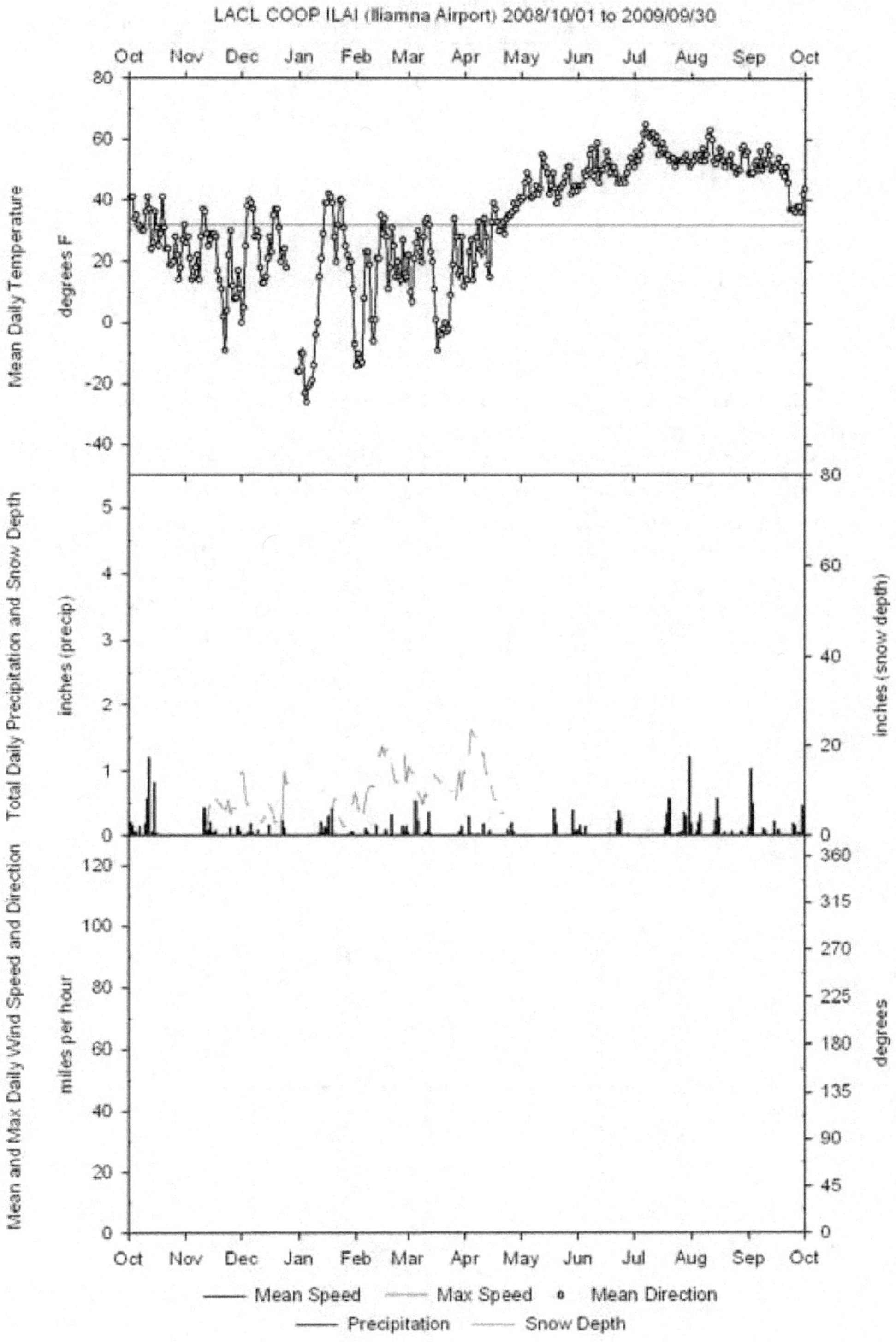

LACL COOP ILAI (Iliamna Airport) 2008/10/01 to 2009/09/30

2009 Hydrologic Year – LACL COOP KEAI (Kenai Airport)

	Oct	Nov	Dec	Jan	Feb	Mar	Apr	May	Jun	Jul	Aug	Sep	Year
Minimum air temperature (°F)													
Min.	5	-4	-29	-34	-23	-16	1	29	35	40	35	24	-34
Max.	41	31	33	36	32	32	38	44	49	56	54	52	56
Mean	24.3	15.1	6.1	2.6	4.4	12	26.5	36.2	43.6	49.7	46.5	40.5	25.7
# days < 32 °F	24	30	28	27	26	29	20	4	0	0	0	2	190
% valid obs	100	100	100	100	100	100	100	100	100	100	100	100	100
Maximum air temperature (°F)													
Min.	27	18	-9	-11	2	20	31	45	52	58	56	45	-11
Max.	55	42	38	46	40	42	63	72	80	73	75	70	80
Mean	39	30.1	20.7	18.6	26	30.6	44.1	58	61.5	65.1	64.2	58.6	43.1
# days < 32 °F	5	17	25	23	17	18	1	0	0	0	0	0	106
% valid obs	100	100	100	100	100	100	100	100	100	100	100	100	100
Mean air temperature (°F)													
Observed	31.6	22.6	13.4	10.5	15.2	21.3	35.2	47.2	52.5	57.4	55.4	49.7	34.4
% valid obs	100	100	100	100	100	100	100	100	100	100	100	100	100
POR mean[1]	34.9	21.8	15.0	12.5	17.2	22.8	34.4	44.2	50.8	54.9	53.9	47.1	34.1
1971-2000	34.3	21.8	16.3	13.4	16.6	23.5	34.6	44.4	50.8	55.0	54.0	46.9	34.3
Precipitation (in)													
Total	2.63	0.34	0.37	1.36	0.54	0.38	0.11	0.68	0.95	1.15	2.3	1.48	12.29
% valid obs	100	100	100	100	100	100	100	100	100	100	100	100	100
POR mean[1]	2.47	1.50	1.35	1.03	0.96	0.83	0.73	0.91	1.19	1.86	2.60	3.32	18.75
1971-2000	2.66	1.69	1.45	1.07	0.91	0.81	0.64	0.95	1.09	1.75	2.62	3.31	18.95
Snow depth (in)													
Average													
% valid obs													
POR mean[1]	1	3	8	12	13	12	3	0	0	0	0	0	
Wind (mph, degrees)													
Mean speed													
% valid obs													
Max speed													
Max direction													
Solar radiation (KWh/m²)													
Total													
% valid obs													

[1]Period of record used: 9/03/1949 to 12/31/2009

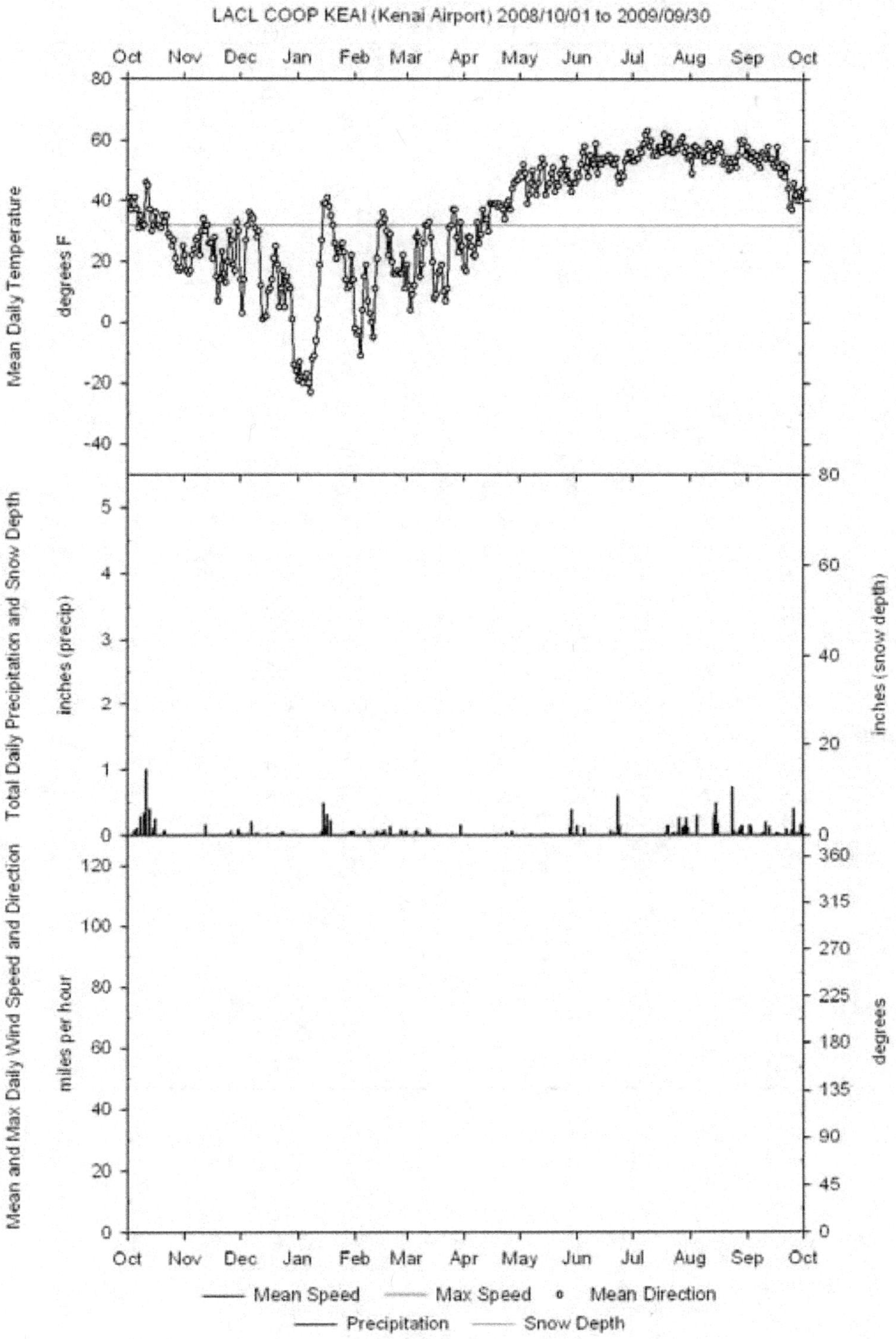

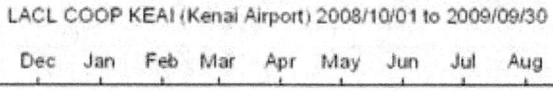

LACL COOP KEAI (Kenai Airport) 2008/10/01 to 2009/09/30

2009 Hydrologic Year – LACL COOP POAL (Port Alsworth)												
	Oct	Nov	Dec	Jan	Feb	Mar	Apr	May	Jun	Jul	Aug	Sep	Year
Minimum air temperature (°F)													
Min.	0	-11		-42	-35	-27	0	23	36	37		27	-42
Max.	37	35		42	32	34	42	46	52	62		51	62
Mean	19.8	9.1		-1.1	3	4.2	24.2	34.3	43	49.1		39.6	22.9
# days < 32 °F	29	29		26	27	29	22	10	0	0		4	176
% valid obs	100	96.7	0	100	92.9	96.8	100	100	100	100	0	100	81.9
Maximum air temperature (°F)													
Min.	21	3		-28	-16	5	27	48	52	60		42	-28
Max.	51	39		52	43	43	64	70	81	85		70	85
Mean	36.3	24.1		15.7	23.4	27.2	44	61.3	64.3	71.7		57.5	42.9
# days < 32 °F	7	20		21	18	16	2	0	0	0		0	84
% valid obs	100	100	0	100	89.3	100	100	100	100	100	0	100	82.2
Mean air temperature (°F)													
Observed	28.1	16.4		7.3	13.4	15.7	34.1	47.9	53.8	60.5		48.6	33.0
% valid obs	100	96.7	0	100	89.3	96.8	100	100	100	100	0	100	81.9
POR mean[1]	34.3	23.7	16.7	14.0	16.9	22.5	33.9	44.8	53.2	57.3	55.2	47.3	35.0
1971-2000	34.5	23.9	17.6	14.7	16.1	23.9	34.9	45.8	54.0	58.3	56.2	47.9	35.7
Precipitation (in)													
Total	1.88	1.31		2.98	1.35	2.08	0.33	0.56	1.21	1.73		2.48	15.93
% valid obs	100	100	0	100	92.9	100	96.7	100	100	100	0	100	82.2
POR mean[1]	1.64	1.38	1.10	0.84	0.69	0.72	0.56	0.54	1.10	1.53	2.36	2.39	14.84
1971-2000	1.37	1.25	1.08	0.79	0.58	0.65	0.48	0.48	0.92	1.40	2.06	2.09	13.15
Snow depth (in)													
Average	2	5		6	9	14	8	0	0	0		0	
% valid obs	96.8	96.7	0	100	96.4	100	100	100	96.7	100	0	86.7	
POR mean[1]	0	3	6	6	6	5	2	0	0	0	0	0	
Wind (mph, degrees)													
Mean speed													
% valid obs													
Max speed													
Max direction													
Solar radiation (KWh/m²)													
Total													
% valid obs													

[1]Period of record used: 7/01/1960 to 12/31/2009

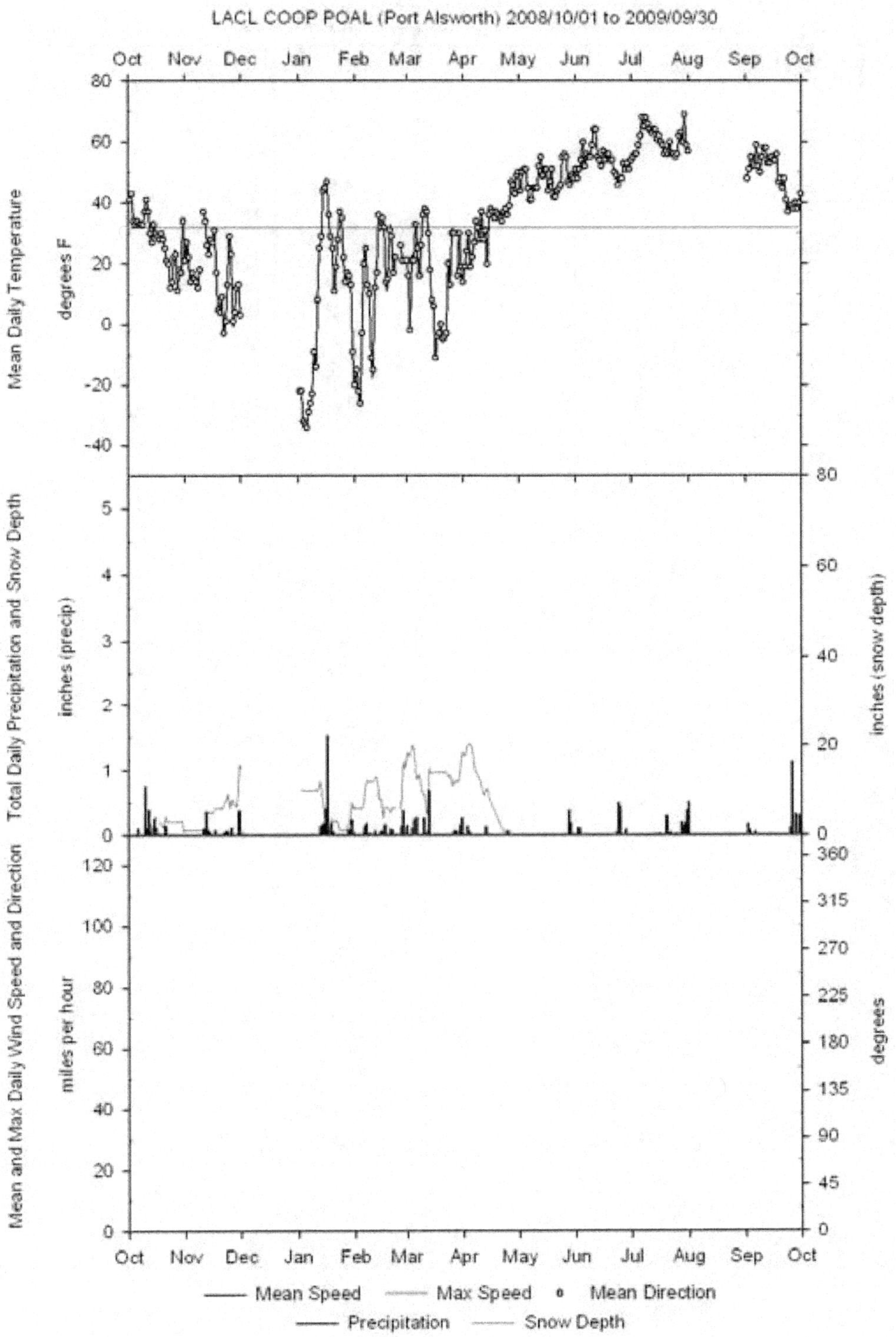

LACL COOP POAL (Port Alsworth) 2008/10/01 to 2009/09/30

2009 Hydrologic Year – LACL COOP TELA (Telaquana Lake)												
	Oct	Nov	Dec	Jan	Feb	Mar	Apr	May	Jun	Jul	Aug	Sep	Year
Minimum air temperature (°F)													
Min.	-1	-28	-43	-50	-46	-31	-3	22	33	41	31	21	-50
Max.	33	31	33	37	34	32	45	42	58	57	59	47	59
Mean	15.2	0.8	-2.2	-9.6	-0.9	-1	23	32.4	42.4	50.6	42.4	36.2	19.2
# days < 32 °F	29	30	30	28	26	30	25	18	0	0	1	8	225
% valid obs	100	100	100	100	100	100	100	100	100	100	100	100	100
Maximum air temperature (°F)													
Min.	4	-16	-35	-42	-22	-8	20	41	49	55	48	33	-42
Max.	44	38	40	51	39	41	62	72	74	83	75	67	83
Mean	26.7	13.7	15.2	6.4	21.3	21.3	38.9	56.9	61	69.5	60.5	52	37
# days < 32 °F	21	27	25	22	20	21	5	0	0	0	0	0	141
% valid obs	100	100	100	100	100	100	100	100	100	100	100	100	100
Mean air temperature (°F)													
Observed	21.2	7.4	6.6	-1.5	10.3	10.3	31.1	44.9	51.9	60.4	51.7	44.4	28.3
% valid obs	100	100	100	100	100	100	100	100	100	100	100	100	100
POR mean 1971-2000													
Precipitation (in)													
Total[2]	0.45	0	0	0.86	0	1.1	0.09	0.87	2.76	0.48	2.11	1.77	10.49
% valid obs													
POR mean 1971-2000													
Snow depth (in)													
Average													
% valid obs													
POR mean													
Wind (mph, degrees)													
Mean speed													
% valid obs													
Max speed													
Max direction													
Solar radiation (KWh/m²)													
Total													
% valid obs													

[2]Station is only capable of measuring liquid precipitation. Percentage of valid observations are not reported for this station.

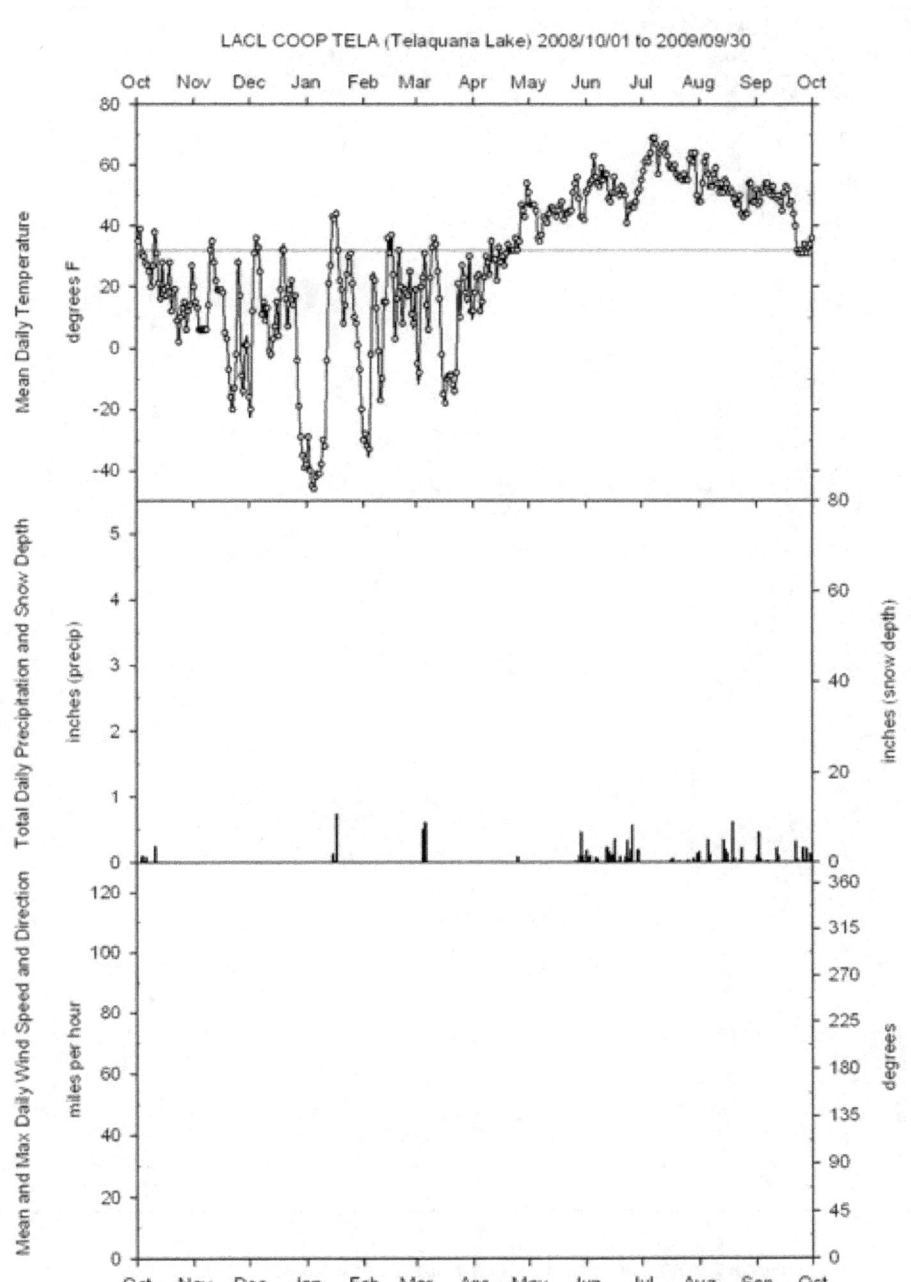

2009 Hydrologic Year – LACL RAWS CHMO (Chigmit Mountains)													
	Oct	Nov	Dec	Jan	Feb	Mar	Apr	May	Jun	Jul	Aug	Sep	Year
Minimum air temperature (°F)													
Min.										32	28.9	16.7	16.7
Max.										55.8	42.8	43.9	55.8
Mean										41.8	36.2	29.5	35.9
# days < 32 °F										0	3	12	15
% valid obs										98.8	97.3	95.1	24.5
Maximum air temperature (°F)													
Min.										34.3	35.8	25.2	25.2
Max.										71.4	54.9	55.9	71.4
Mean										51.2	45.1	37.3	44.6
# days < 32 °F										0	0	9	9
% valid obs										98.8	97.3	95.1	24.5
Mean air temperature (°F)													
Observed										45.7	40	33.1	39.8
% valid obs										98.8	97.6	95.6	24.5
POR mean													
1971-2000													
Precipitation (in)													
Total[2]										18.4	4.6	9.69	32.69
% valid obs										94.4	97.2	69.3	22
POR mean													
1971-2000													
Snow depth (in)													
Average													
% valid obs													
POR mean													
Wind (mph, degrees)													
Mean speed										16.8	12.5	13.4	
% valid obs										98.8	97.6	96	
Max speed										88.8	62	68.7	88.8
Max direction										81	116	94	81
Solar radiation (KWh/m[2])													
Total										152.8	130	60.3	343
% valid obs										98.8	97.3	95.1	24.5

[2]Station is only capable of measuring liquid precipitation. Precipitation reported when maximum air temperature is below 31.1 °F is not considered valid and these data are not used for summarizing purposes. The water equivalent of solid precipitation (e.g. snowfall) is not measured and this is reflected in the percentage of valid observations that are reported as a measure of the reliability of cumulative values.

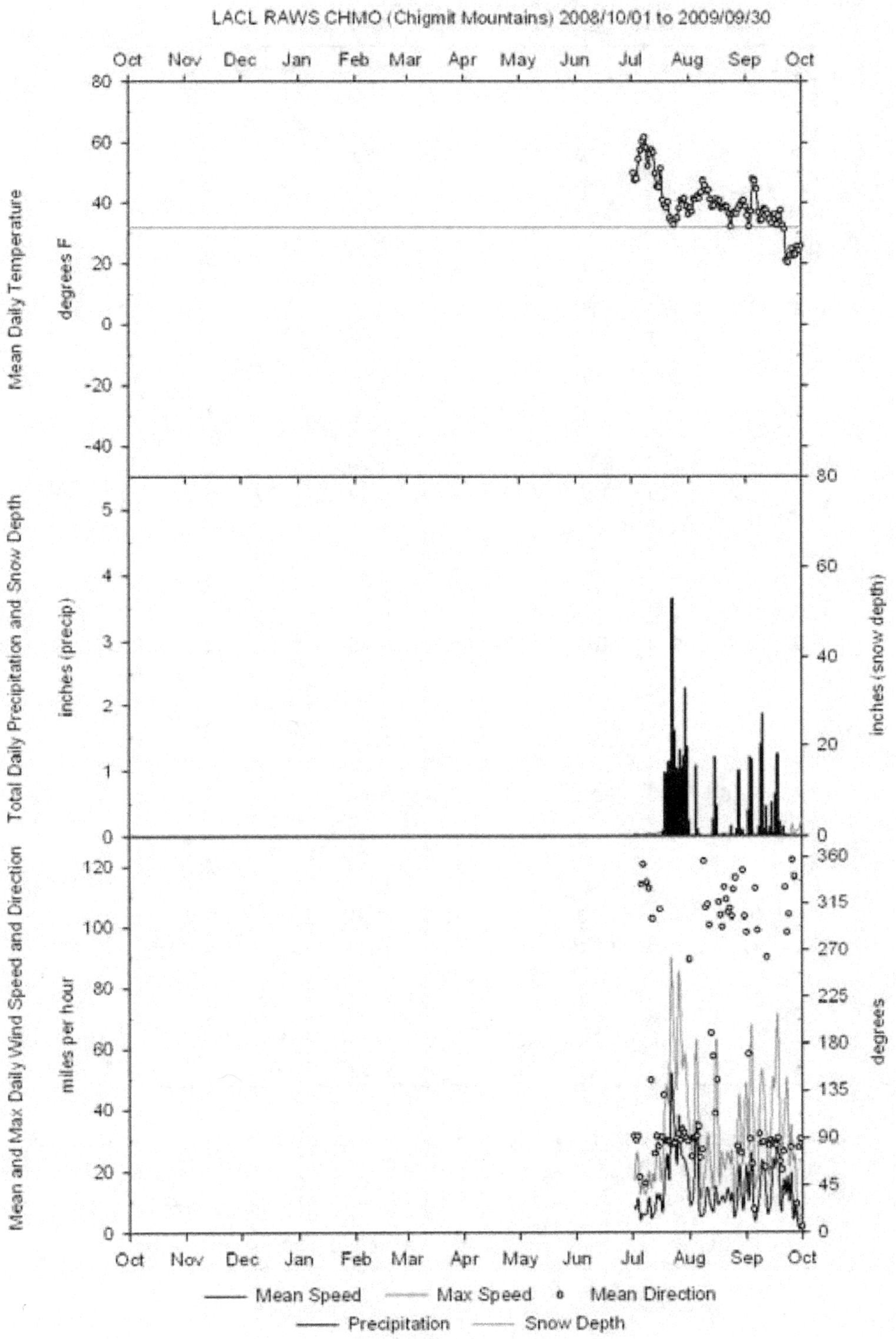

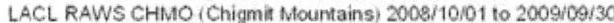

LACL RAWS CHMO (Chigmit Mountains) 2008/10/01 to 2009/09/30

2009 Hydrologic Year – LACL RAWS HILA (Hickerson Lake)												
---	Oct	Nov	Dec	Jan	Feb	Mar	Apr	May	Jun	Jul	Aug	Sep	Year
Minimum air temperature (°F)													
Min.	18.5	10.6	2.8	-6.5	-6.5	3.2	15.4	31.3	37.9	43.2	41.5	32.2	-6.5
Max.	36.5	30.4	34.3	34.2	29.3	28	36.7	49.6	49.8	63.3	52.9	49.3	63.3
Mean	27.9	21.5	19.4	15.3	15.6	16.5	28.5	39.7	42.2	49.3	47.3	43.1	30.6
# days < 32 °F	23	30	28	28	28	31	20	1	0	0	0	0	189
% valid obs	100	100	100	100	100	100	100	100	98.5	99.7	99.7	100	99.8
Maximum air temperature (°F)													
Min.	28.2	21	11.3	6.3	8.1	16	28.8	38.7	45	49.6	49.8	39.6	6.3
Max.	49.8	36.9	36.9	44.2	39.6	45.1	54.7	72.1	73.6	80.6	69.3	66.6	80.6
Mean	38.2	30.5	27.2	25.3	27.5	29.3	40.5	54.6	57.1	61.8	60.3	52.4	42.1
# days < 32 °F	3	18	23	20	18	22	2	0	0	0	0	0	106
% valid obs	100	100	100	100	100	100	100	100	98.5	99.7	99.7	100	99.8
Mean air temperature (°F)													
Observed	32.2	25.7	23.1	20.1	21	22.5	33.4	46.8	49.1	55.3	53.1	47.2	35.9
% valid obs	100	100	100	100	100	100	100	100	98.5	99.7	99.7	100	99.8
POR mean													
1971-2000													
Precipitation (in)													
Total[2]	1.93	0.53	0.45	3.13	0.61	0.47	1.73	5.62	2.67	9.69	5.57	5.51	37.91
% valid obs	100	100	100	100	100	100	100	100	98.3	99.7	99.9	100	99.8
POR mean													
1971-2000													
Snow depth (in)													
Average	0.5	4.2	5.9	6.2	13.6	26.4	20.3	1	0.2	0.2	0.4	0.4	
% valid obs	98.9	99.6	100	92.9	100	98.5	99.4	98.3	97.6	84.7	96	93.9	
POR mean													
Wind (mph, degrees)													
Mean speed	10.6	12.9	13.9	14	9.9	12.4	11.2	7.2	5.3	9.3	7.8	12.4	
% valid obs	100	100	100	100	100	100	100	21.9	4.4	99.7	99.7	100	
Max speed	60.2	72.3	84.8	60.2	54.8	75.4	50.1	33.3	14.3	93.3	75.8	88.8	93.3
Max direction	3	1	10	60	336	14	0	6	186	0	5	9	0
Solar radiation (KWh/m²)													
Total	45.7	13.5	7.1	11.9	32.2	76.4	118.4	161.2	151.3	133.2	119.6	63.9	934.2
% valid obs	100	100	100	100	100	100	100	100	98.5	99.7	99.9	100	99.8

[2]Station is only capable of measuring liquid precipitation. Precipitation reported when maximum air temperature is below 31.1 °F is not considered valid and these data are not used for summarizing purposes. The water equivalent of solid precipitation (e.g. snowfall) is not measured and this is reflected in the percentage of valid observations that are reported as a measure of the reliability of cumulative values.

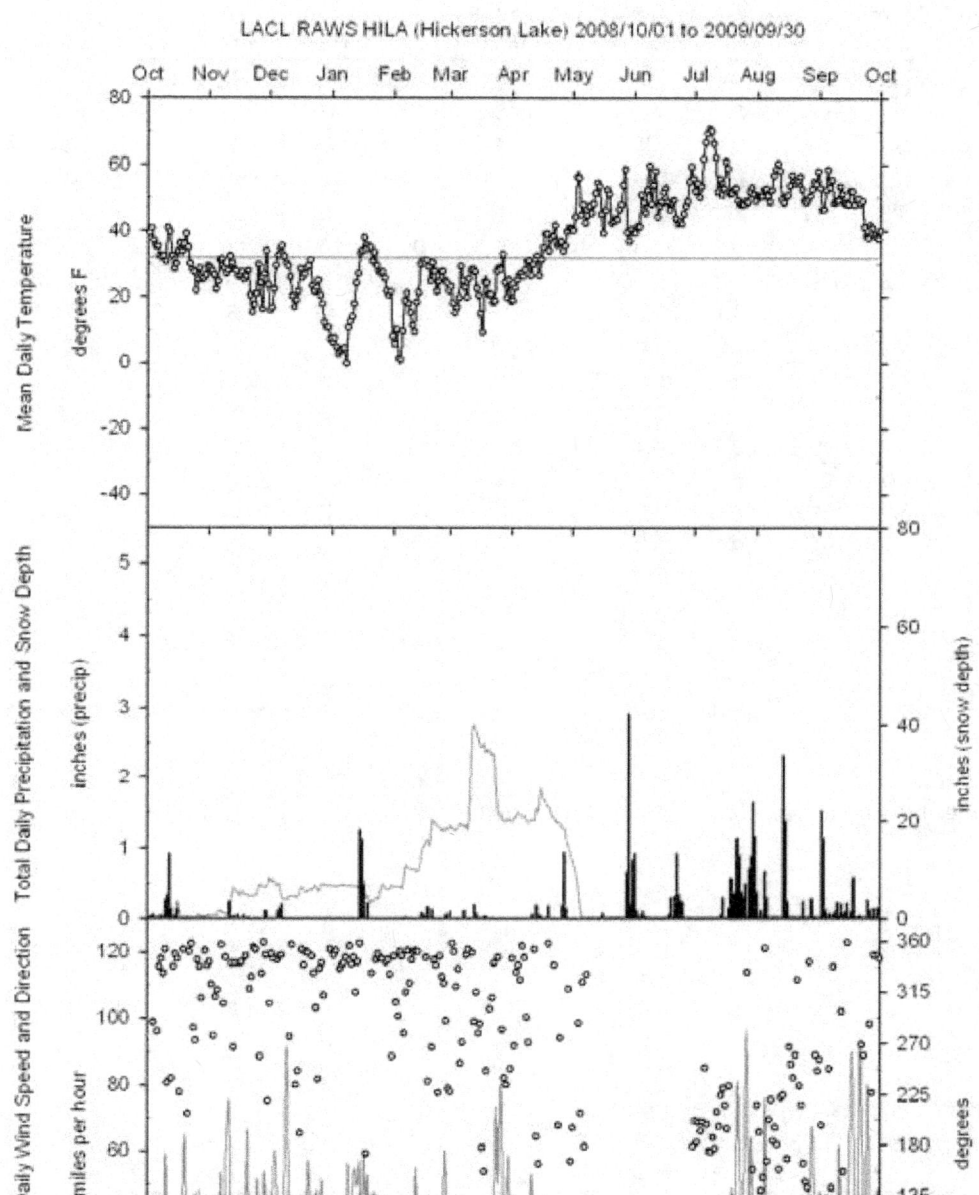

LACL RAWS HILA (Hickerson Lake) 2008/10/01 to 2009/09/30

2009 Hydrologic Year – LACL RAWS POAL (Port Alsworth)

	Oct	Nov	Dec	Jan	Feb	Mar	Apr	May	Jun	Jul	Aug	Sep	Year
Minimum air temperature (°F)													
Min.	-4	-14	-30	-41		-8	1	19	30	35	29	24	-41
Max.	34	34	38	41		33	42	43	48	56	54	47	56
Mean	17.2	8.3	8.2	-0.9		11.6	22.8	30.3	38.8	47.5	41.9	36.4	25
# days < 32 °F	28	29	27	24		6	26	20	2	0	2	8	172
% valid obs	100	99.9	99.7	89.4	0	20.6	100	100	100	99.7	100	100	84.6
Maximum air temperature (°F)													
Min.	23	-3	-19	-29		22	29	46	56	57	56	39	-29
Max.	51	41	44	54		42	69	74	85	88	78	71	88
Mean	36.2	23.6	23.1	16.4		33.7	46.3	62.5	66.2	72.8	67.5	57.5	47.2
# days < 32 °F	7	18	19	20		3	1	0	0	0	0	0	68
% valid obs	100	99.9	99.7	89.4	0	20.6	100	100	100	99.7	100	100	84.6
Mean air temperature (°F)													
Observed	27.1	15.8	16.5	7.2		22.9	34.9	47.6	53.4	60.9	54.7	46.7	36.5
% valid obs	100	99.9	99.7	89.4	0	20.6	100	100	100	99.7	100	100	84.6
POR mean													
1971-2000													
Precipitation (in)													
Total[2]	1.55	0.27	0.83	2.31		0.04	0.58	0.52	1.31	1.66	1.16	1.67	11.9
% valid obs	37.8	16	25.4	20.4	0	5.5	62.4	86.2	99.6	99.7	99.3	94.6	54.2
POR mean													
1971-2000													
Snow depth (in)													
Average													
% valid obs													
POR mean													
Wind (mph, degrees)													
Mean speed				1.2		5	3.2	2.7	2.6	3.5	2.3	2.2	
% valid obs	0	0	0	6.6	0	20.6	100	100	100	99.7	100	100	
Max speed				11		31	26	19	22	28	23	21	31
Max direction				30		77	73	122	93	91	77	62	77
Solar radiation (KWh/m^2)													
Total	39.2	12.3	2.5	4	0	15.4	134.3	199.6	187	174.8	138.7	80	987.8
% valid obs	100	99.9	99.7	89.4	0	20.6	100	100	100	99.7	100	100	84.6

[2]Station is only capable of measuring liquid precipitation. Precipitation reported when maximum air temperature is below 31.1 °F is not considered valid and these data are not used for summarizing purposes. The water equivalent of solid precipitation (e.g. snowfall) is not measured and this is reflected in the percentage of valid observations that are reported as a measure of the reliability of cumulative values.

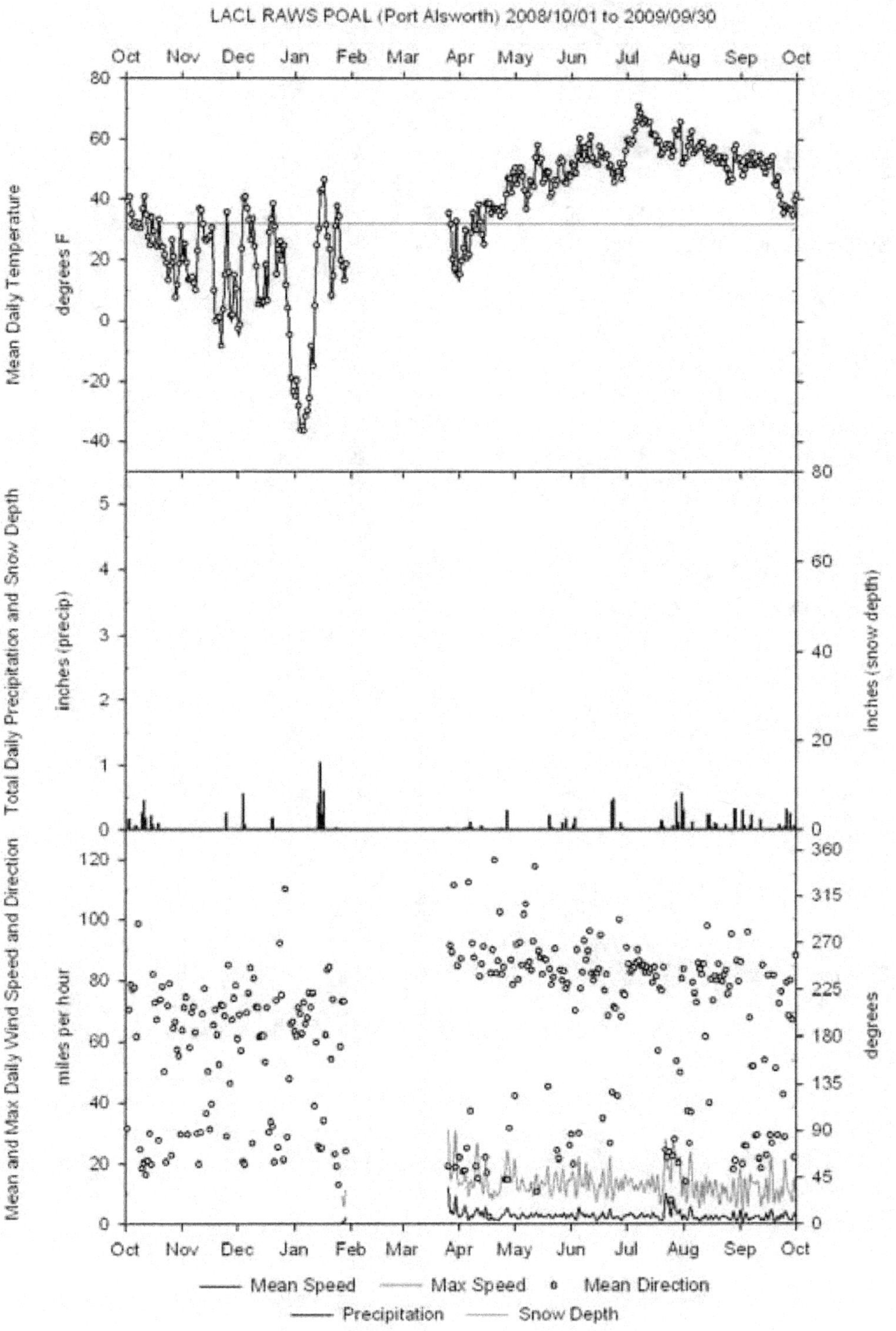

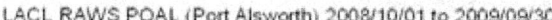

LACL RAWS POAL (Port Alsworth) 2008/10/01 to 2009/09/30
Oct Nov Dec Jan Feb Mar Apr May Jun Jul Aug Sep Oct
Mean Daily Temperature
degrees F
80 60 40 20 0 -20 -40
Total Daily Precipitation and Snow Depth
inches (precip)
5 4 3 2 1 0
inches (snow depth)
80 60 40 20 0
Mean and Max Daily Wind Speed and Direction
miles per hour
120 100 80 60 40 20 0
degrees
360 315 270 225 180 135 90 45 0
Mean Speed
Max Speed
Mean Direction
Precipitation
Snow Depth

2009 Hydrologic Year – LACL RAWS SNLA (Snipe Lake)	Oct	Nov	Dec	Jan	Feb	Mar	Apr	May	Jun	Jul	Aug	Sep	Year
Minimum air temperature (°F)													
Min.	-2.9	-19.7	-21.6	-34.1	-27.9	-25.6	2.7	23.9	34.7	39.9	33.6	22.6	-34.1
Max.	32.5	27.1	32.5	32	27.3	27.9	43.7	45.5	50.9	60.4	52.9	48	60.4
Mean	14.9	5.4	10.6	2.8	5.6	3.2	23	35.4	41.4	50.3	43.1	36.9	22.8
# days < 32 °F	30	30	29	30	28	31	25	7	0	0	0	10	220
% valid obs	100	100	100	100	100	100	100	100	99.7	99.7	100	99.9	99.9
Maximum air temperature (°F)													
Min.	9.9	-4.4	-14.6	-22.9	-17.7	-15	17.1	35.1	46.4	50	45.7	29.1	-22.9
Max.	41.7	34	39	43.5	34.9	42.1	54.5	68.9	73.8	80.4	65.7	66.2	80.4
Mean	28.7	18.4	21.5	15.7	21	18.7	35.5	53.4	56.7	64.4	57.4	49.1	36.8
# days < 32 °F	19	29	20	24	24	28	10	0	0	0	0	2	156
% valid obs	100	100	100	100	100	100	100	100	99.7	99.7	100	99.9	99.9
Mean air temperature (°F)													
Observed	21	11.6	16.1	9.1	13.2	11.2	29.3	44.2	48.7	57.4	49.7	42.1	29.5
% valid obs	100	100	100	100	100	100	100	100	99.7	99.7	100	99.9	99.9
POR mean 1971-2000													
Precipitation (in)													
Total[2]	0.64	0	0.03	0.54	0.01	0.79	0.47	1.15	2.29	1.24	1.54	1.43	10.13
% valid obs	16.9	2.1	21.8	16	4.8	5	42.9	96.9	99.6	99.7	100	83.6	49.4
POR mean 1971-2000													
Snow depth (in)													
Average	1.7	1.3	0.4	1.6	1.2	0.3	0.4	0.1	0.1	0.2	0.2	0.9	
% valid obs	86.4	99.2	92.7	91.4	94.3	90.9	59.3	11.8	68.3	88.8	89.4	90.7	
POR mean													
Wind (mph, degrees)													
Mean speed	8.2	8.3	10.9	11.7	11.7	12.7	11.8	10.1	10.2	14.2	9.5	8.7	
% valid obs	100	100	100	100	100	100	100	100	99.7	99.7	100	99.9	
Max speed	62	46.5	73.6	86.6	70.5	75.4	48.3	41.4	55.7	56.2	46.1	37.8	86.6
Max direction	118	107	116	121	124	120	127	117	113	110	109	91	121
Solar radiation (KWh/m^2)													
Total	35	14.1	5	9	26.8	81.4	129.2	170.4	145.4	150	112.7	66.9	945.9
% valid obs	100	100	100	100	100	100	100	100	99.7	99.7	100	99.9	99.9

[2]Station is only capable of measuring liquid precipitation. Precipitation reported when maximum air temperature is below 31.1 °F is not considered valid and these data are not used for summarizing purposes. The water equivalent of solid precipitation (e.g. snowfall) is not measured and this is reflected in the percentage of valid observations that are reported as a measure of the reliability of cumulative values.

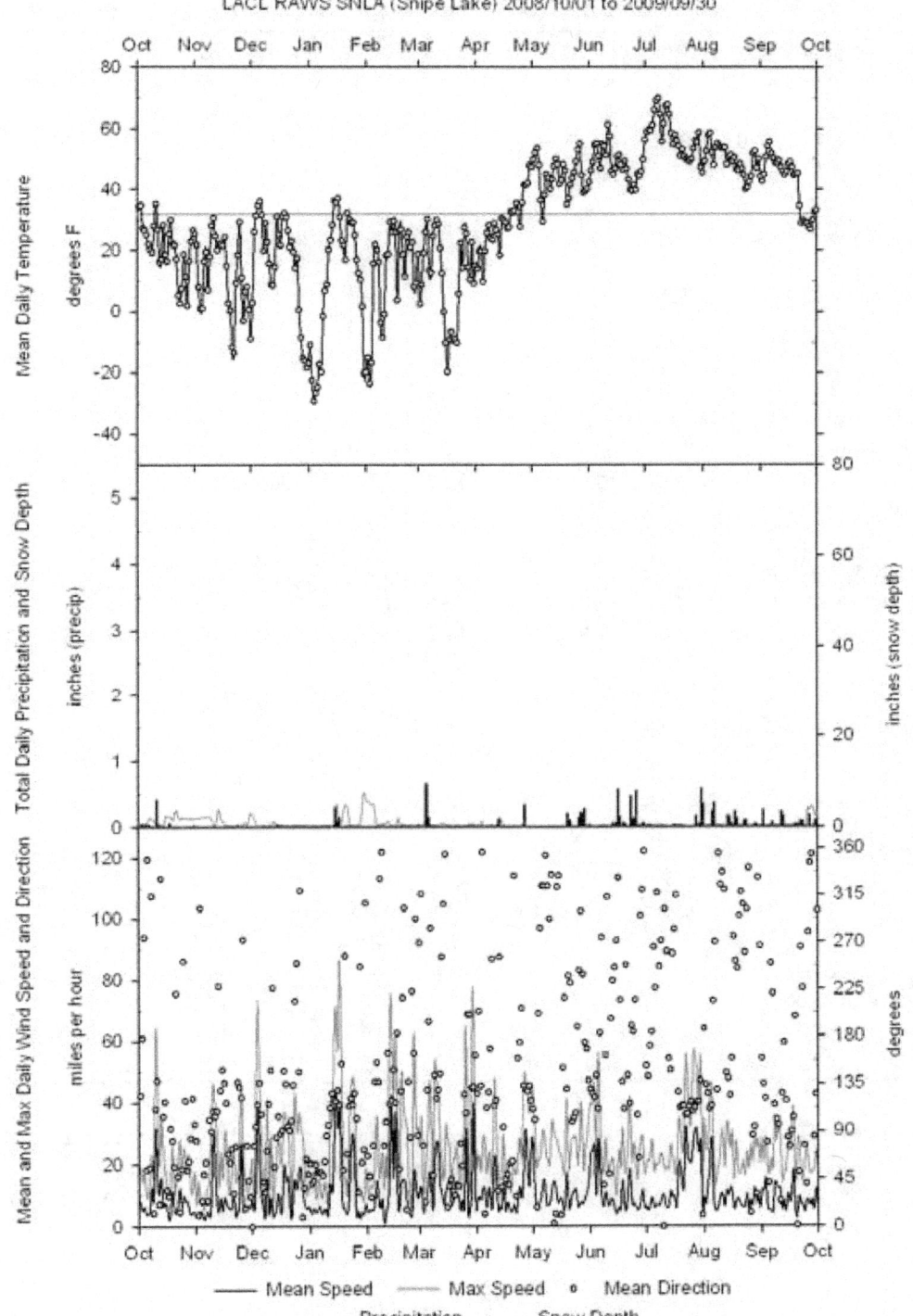

LACL RAWS SNLA (Snipe Lake) 2008/10/01 to 2009/09/30

2009 Hydrologic Year – LACL RAWS STON (Stoney)												
	Oct	Nov	Dec	Jan	Feb	Mar	Apr	May	Jun	Jul	Aug	Sep	Year
Minimum air temperature (°F)													
Min.	-18	-36	-46	-55	-46	-40	-11	12	28	32	25	8	-55
Max.	31	24	33	37	34	31	31	42	47	56	53	44	56
Mean	5.7	-7.6	-6.8	-12.9	-4.5	-4	17.4	26.8	37.9	45.1	36.7	29.4	13.7
# days < 32 °F	31	30	30	29	27	31	30	25	7	0	12	17	269
% valid obs	100	100	99.9	100	100	98.4	100	100	100	99.9	100	100	99.8
Maximum air temperature (°F)													
Min.	7	-12	-31	-36	-14	-3	26	47	54	56	51	34	-36
Max.	48	40	39	51	40	41	69	80	83	90	79	73	90
Mean	28.7	14.4	14.1	7.7	22.9	24.7	43.9	62.7	66	74.4	66	56	40.2
# days < 32 °F	18	26	27	23	17	21	2	0	0	0	0	0	134
% valid obs	100	100	99.9	100	100	98.4	100	100	100	99.9	100	100	99.8
Mean air temperature (°F)													
Observed	17.4	4.2	3.9	-3.7	9.4	11.6	31.8	46.9	52.8	61.5	52.3	42.5	27.7
% valid obs	100	100	99.9	100	100	98.4	100	100	100	99.9	100	100	99.8
POR mean													
1971-2000													
Precipitation (in)													
Total[2]	0.48	0.02	0.09	1.5	0.02	0.45	0.43	0.8	3.02	0.85	1.75	1.49	10.9
% valid obs	14.2	7.1	6.6	15.5	15.2	13.2	51.7	83.7	97.5	99.9	94.9	78.2	48.3
POR mean													
1971-2000													
Snow depth (in)													
Average													
% valid obs													
POR mean													
Wind (mph, degrees)													
Mean speed	1.2	0.8	0.8	1.5	2.7	3.6	3.4	3.6	3.2	4.1	3.2	2.6	
% valid obs	100	100	99.9	100	100	98.4	100	100	100	99.9	100	100	
Max speed	36	27	37	44	29	34	25	21	28	32	22	22	44
Max direction	354	30	14	105	201	30	0	243	150	9	6	5	105
Solar radiation (KWh/m[2])													
Total	35	14.1	5	9	26.8	81.4	129.2	170.4	145.4	150	112.7	66.9	968.4
% valid obs	100	100	100	100	100	100	100	100	99.7	99.7	100	99.9	99.8

[2]Station is only capable of measuring liquid precipitation. Precipitation reported when maximum air temperature is below 31.1 °F is not considered valid and these data are not used for summarizing purposes. The water equivalent of solid precipitation (e.g. snowfall) is not measured and this is reflected in the percentage of valid observations that are reported as a measure of the reliability of cumulative values.

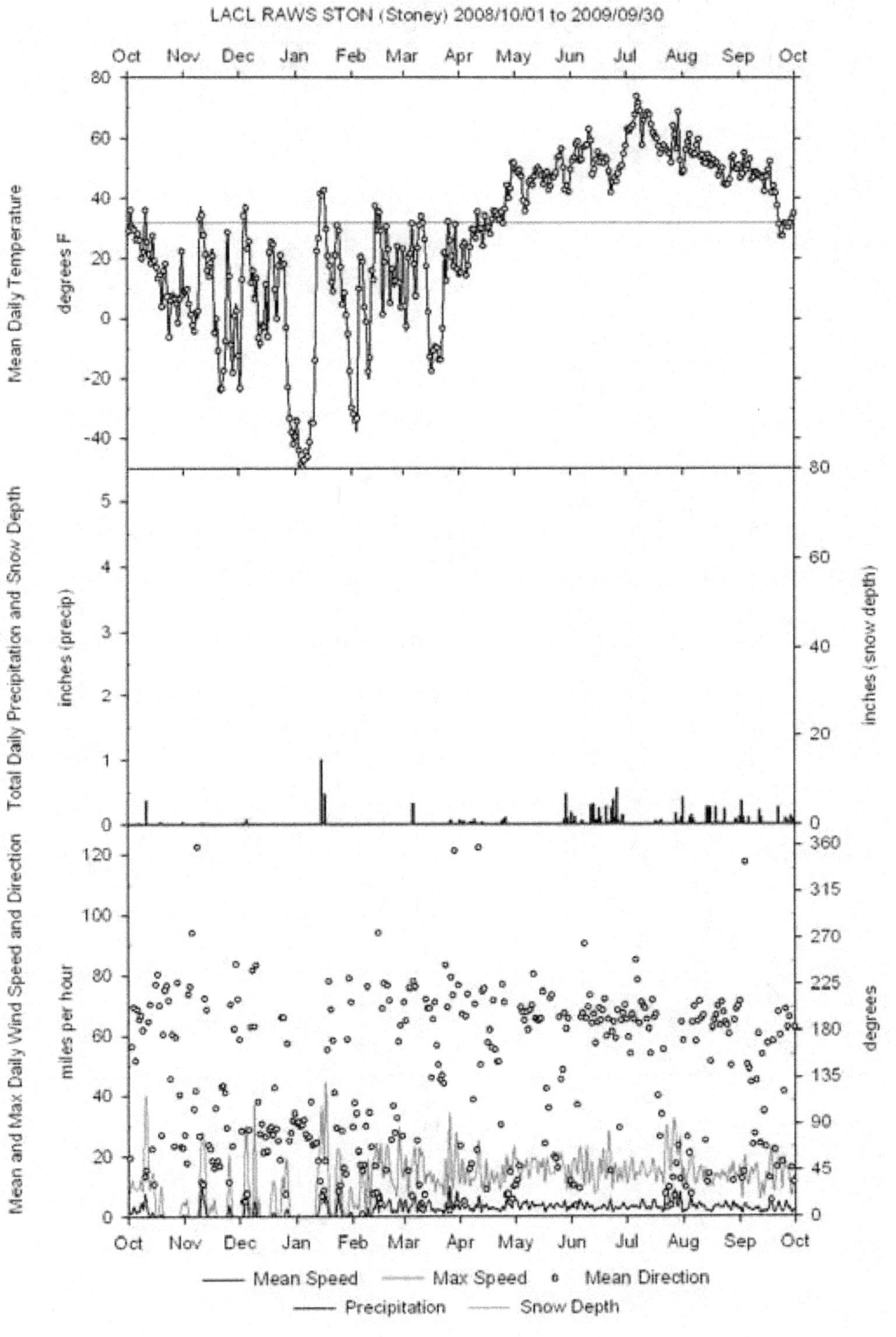

LACL RAWS STON (Stoney) 2008/10/01 to 2009/09/30

2009 Hydrologic Year – LACL SNCO POAL (Port Alsworth)													
	Oct	Nov	Dec	Jan	Feb	Mar	Apr	May	Jun	Jul	Aug	Sep	Year
Minimum air temperature (°F)													
Min.													
Max.													
Mean													
# days < 32 °F													
% valid obs													
Maximum air temperature (°F)													
Min.													
Max.													
Mean													
# days < 32 °F													
% valid obs													
Mean air temperature (°F)													
Observed													
% valid obs													
POR mean													
1971-2000													
Precipitation (in)													
Total[3]						5.2	6.8						
% valid obs						100	100						
POR mean													
1971-2000													
Snow depth (in)													
Average[4]						22	28						
% valid obs						100	100						
POR mean													
Wind (mph, degrees)													
Mean speed													
% valid obs													
Max speed													
Max direction													
Solar radiation (KWh/m[2])													
Total													
% valid obs													

[3]Snow water equivalent measured close to the beginning of the month.
[4]Cumulative snow depth measured close to the beginning of the month.

LACL SNCO POAL (Port Alsworth) 2008/10/01 to 2009/09/30

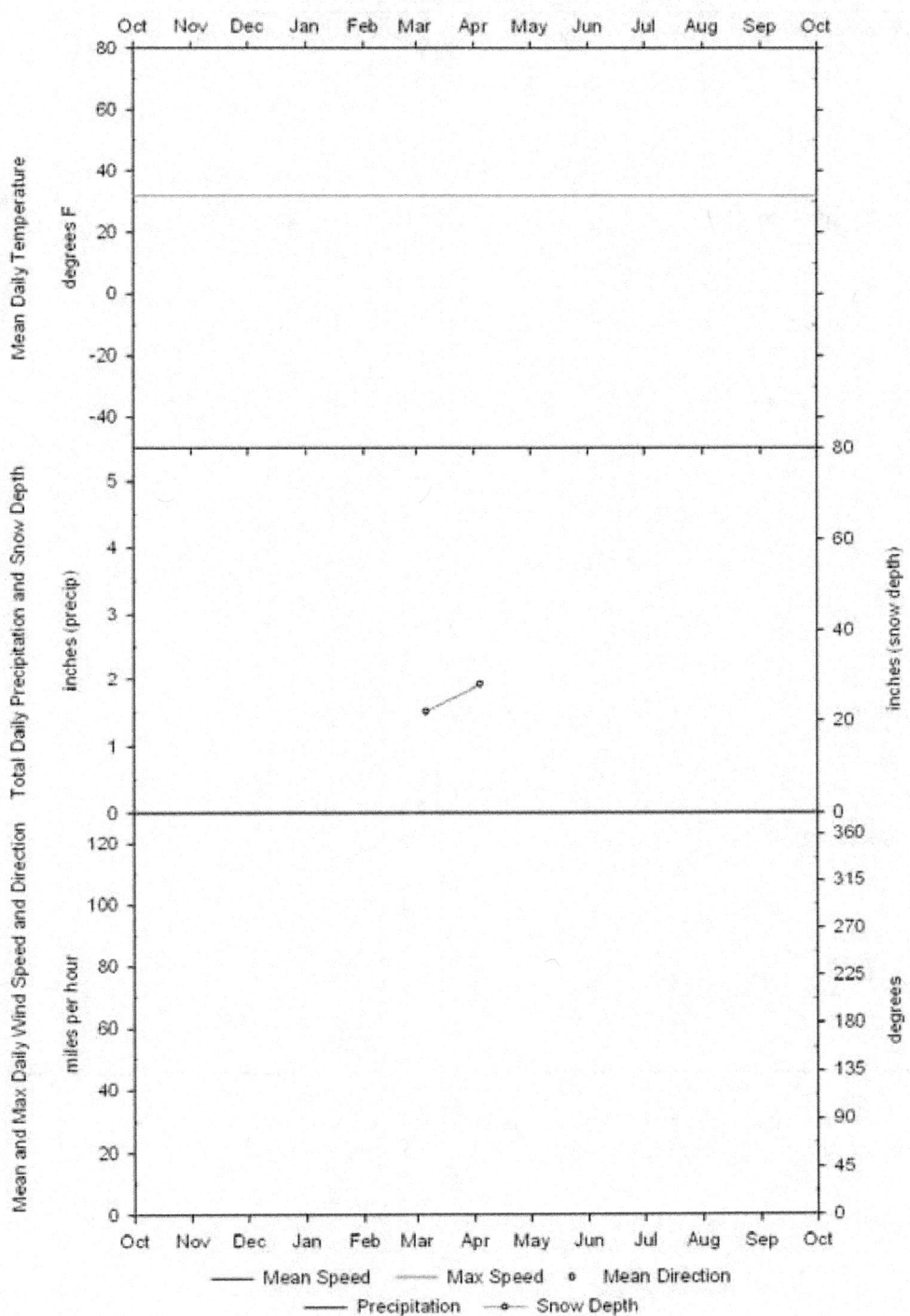

2009 Hydrologic Year – LACL SNCO TELA (Telaquana Lake)	Oct	Nov	Dec	Jan	Feb	Mar	Apr	May	Jun	Jul	Aug	Sep	Year
Minimum air temperature (°F)													
Min.													
Max.													
Mean													
# days < 32 °F													
% valid obs													
Maximum air temperature (°F)													
Min.													
Max.													
Mean													
# days < 32 °F													
% valid obs													
Mean air temperature (°F)													
Observed													
% valid obs													
POR mean													
1971-2000													
Precipitation (in)													
Total[3]						5.5	6.9	0					
% valid obs						100	100	100					
POR mean													
1971-2000													
Snow depth (in)													
Average[4]						26	23	0					
% valid obs						100	100	100					
POR mean													
Wind (mph, degrees)													
Mean speed													
% valid obs													
Max speed													
Max direction													
Solar radiation (KWh/m²)													
Total													
% valid obs													

[3]Snow water equivalent measured close to the beginning of the month.
[4]Cumulative snow depth measured close to the beginning of the month.

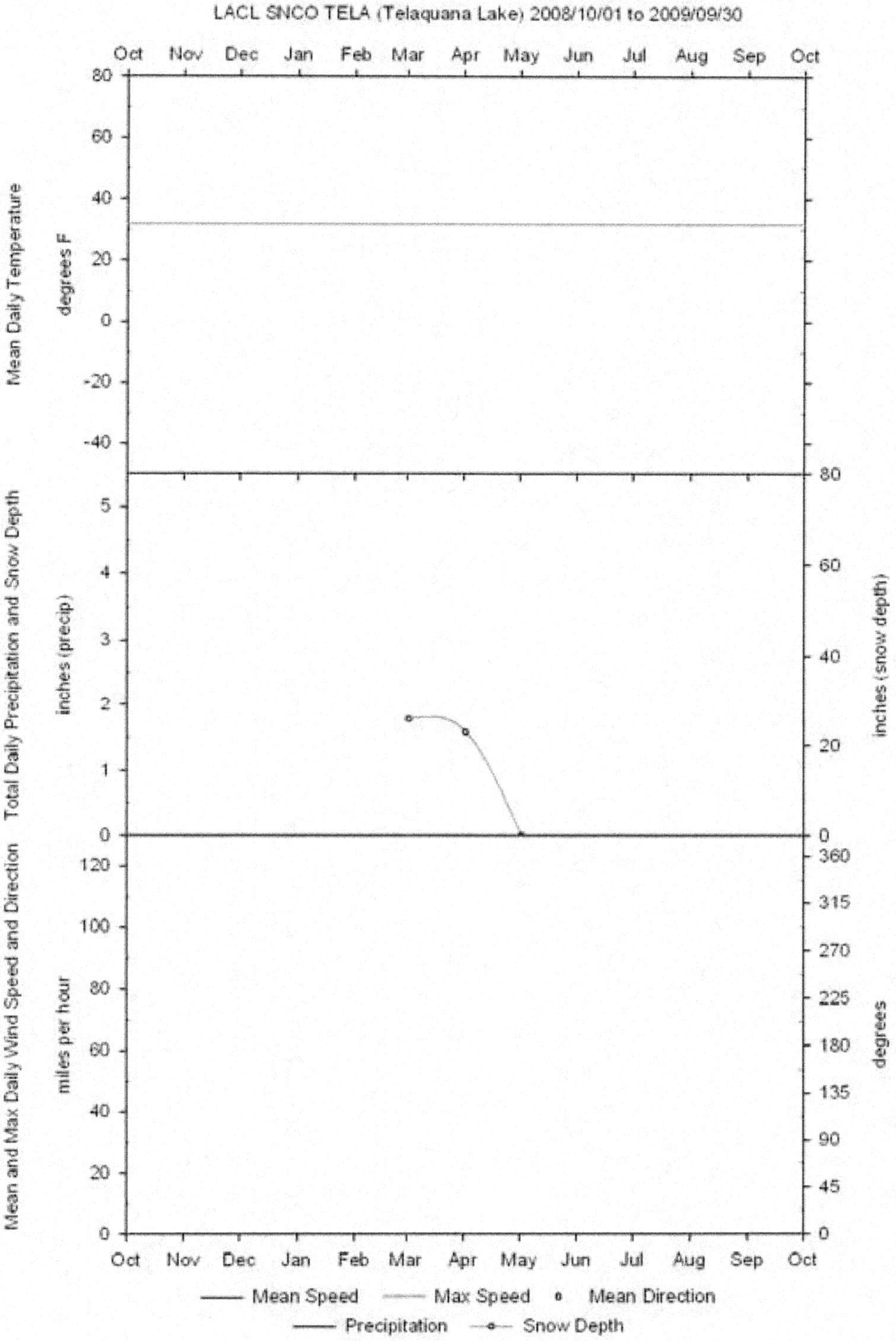

LACL SNCO TELA (Telaquana Lake) 2008/10/01 to 2009/09/30
Oct Nov Dec Jan Feb Mar Apr May Jun Jul Aug Sep Oct
Mean Daily Temperature
degrees F
80 60 40 20 0 -20 -40
Total Daily Precipitation and Snow Depth
inches (precip)
5 4 3 2 1 0
inches (snow depth)
80 60 40 20 0
Mean and Max Daily Wind Speed and Direction
miles per hour
120 100 80 60 40 20 0
degrees
360 315 270 225 180 135 90 45 0
Mean Speed
Max Speed
Mean Direction
Precipitation
Snow Depth

NPS 953/103378, June 2010

National Park Service
U.S. Department of the Interior

Natural Resource Program Center
1201 Oakridge Drive, Suite 150
Fort Collins, CO 80525

www.nature.nps.gov

EXPERIENCE YOUR AMERICA ™

www.ingramcontent.com/pod-product-compliance
Lightning Source LLC
Chambersburg PA
CBHW081111290526

45795CB00006B/2078